Prologue
This is a book compromising of beautiful poems written by the author
short tales narrated by saints from the past which have been lost in
the sands of time rivived in the words of the author and the opening
of secrets of this world and this universe the truth which is hidden
and is portrayed as falsehood is brought to light by the author all
the controversies that surround this creation is portrayed for the
readers to go through the mind of the author and find there own
understanding of what is true and what is false in this universe and
this world increase your knowledge and enjoy the beautiful tales and
have a greater understanding of the past and the future in the last
days of this world.

PART A

Chapter 1-Child

Chapter 2-Cut open

Chapter 3-Diciplined

Chapter 4-Grey

Chapter 5-Holocaust

Chapter 6-House

Chapter 7-Intentions

Chapter 8-Light

Chapter 9-Warmth of a mother

Chapter 10-Saint

Chapter 11-Silence

Chapter 12-Smile

Chapter 13-Spider

Chapter 14-Truth

Chapter 15-Winter

PART B

Chapter 1)Armourgadon.

Chapter 2)Big boss and the grey state.

Chapter 3)Communism.

1) CHILD

As one sees a piece of bread in need
lost in a world filled with greed

overwhelmed by sorrow filled with creed

As the stomach aches the heart prays
holding on to that innocence
as the world lets it drown in the bays

When did life become so grey
father and mother i want to go
back to those days.

2)   CUT OPEN

We were cut open
We were torn apart
But we stiched ourselves back together
And came back stronger than ever

What begins must come to an end
What was can never be again
Just have faith and take gods name
All is in his domain

We beleive so we flourish
We disbelieve and we shall perish
In the end its all the same
Where it started there it shall end

3)   DECIPLINED.

Let the decipline be the cure
Let your soul be pure
A path taken was never meant to be forsaken
Through humiliation one is lead to salvation
Dont let your heart become stone
Learn to make atone
Only through gods will
You will be among the ones in thrill
The illusions of this material abode
Will make you dilusioned
Let it all go have faith in the flow
and bow to the one who made you grow.

4)   GREY.

As one sees a piece of bread in need
Lost in a world filled with greed
Overwhelmed by sorrow filled with creed

As the stomache aches the heart prays
Holding on to that innocence
while the devil designs his plays

When did life become so grey
Just hold on
Dont turn away from your ways

Lord is watching through your pain
Get up and go through it again
Dont let it all go in vain

5)   Holocaust.

We keep trying and at times we see the light at the end of the
tunnel only to realise its just a mirage formed by the blisters of
hope our heart still clings on too again we feel lost in the dark
mazes of loneliness and sorrow where there is absolutely nobody that
is willing to light the candle of hope to show us the way out of
this dark hole we cant escape from.

 we see our freinds our family they seem so close yet are always
 too far we scream for help till we cant no more but our voices are
 always devoured by the demons that wont let go.

It makes us wonder what have we been doing our whole lives was
anything even real feelings of hate seem to overwhelm us for
everything and everyone around us then we feel like letting go of
everyone and everything and be lost into the nothingness which life
has become break the chains of deception hovering over our reality
and the false meanings of life which we have come to rely upon but
then we open our eyes and the harsh realisation hits us we have
already fallen too deep to ever have a chance to climb out.

The voices which surround us keep screaming some recite the verses
from Hell while others sing the choirs of heaven we listen to both
unaware at times where its coming from we try to discover the source
of its creation which leads us astray into oblivion.

We keep reminiscing the past to remember the times laughter filled
our hearts then we face the present and are drowned by the holocast
then we look into the future and cant determine wether its lost.

6)   House.
The house is as stable as
the base it stands on
which is as secure as the
ideas it is build upon
if it is to come down
it must be brought down
by the whispers initiated at its core
rather than the outside browls.

7)   INTENTIONS
The Lord sees efforts and intentions,
not effects of conclusions.

The judgement of humans come upon outcomes,
The judgement of God depends upon endeavours.

Let go off all the dependence   on the worldly
existance,

As we came empty handed and though shall we return.

8) LIGHT.
Let the light be your guide
lose your pride
let faith be your stride

shivering in pain
you lose your gains
Let love be your new lane

following the path of saints
we wish to reach the eternal
world and walk away from the material
existance filled with feint

9) Warmth of a mother
In the days of old
young girls were buried alive
By men considered bold

Then were revealed the words of god
Come to the rightous path
else face the wrath of your lord

The rightly guided followed
By ignorance the rest were swallowed

sweet sister may you grow
like the lion roars
and may happiness fill your soul
like the angel soars

The mothers love is pure
as she sees her childs smile
All her pains find a cure

10) Saint
Everything is temporary
so quit your worries
dont be in a hurry
or you will fall in the quarry.

All that comes to be
will come to an end,
just jump in your train and let
the railroad guide you through

the pain.

In the end you will have to follow
your own lane or else you will go insane,
not everyone can be a saint.

11)   SILENCE.
From silence to violence
how does one go
from lies comes cries
so the rivers of vile may flow

sweet sister may you grow
like the lion roars
and may happiness fill your soul
like eves return to the garden of the old

Dont embrace the past
no goodness will it sow
just let it all go
and it shall pass like the winter blows

12)   SMILE

Greet life with a smile it will change the world around you.

Look at problems as opportunities it will remove the negativity
inside you.

Depend only on the one above you and help the ones beside you.

Appreciate the things you have instead of remenising about the
things you lost
As one day what you have now will be replaced and become what you
have lost.

Dont keep looking back at the past you will miss the present and be
lost in the future.

13)   All is one One is all
As one walks on a path fabricated on the webs of a spider clinging
to superficial worldly illusions of predominant optimism unable to
see the duplicity of ones vicinity living in ignorance of ones maker

One forgets the pupose of ones existance
one forgets the values of ones virtue
one neglects the truth in search of ones pleasures
and disobeys the commands of ones creator

As ones soul is stained with acts of sin
one forgets ones return to where one came from.

14)   Truth
Every human that came before us and every human that comes after us
there are some questions that have been asked before us and will be
asked after we are no more
where did we come from ?
What are we doing here ?
where are we going ?

As death is the absolute truth that none can deny
and for beleivers death is waking up to reality and freeing
ourselves from the bonds of this worldly existance but dont we all
find ourselves asking the same question when we wake up will it
truly be a better place or another corrupted existance.
We reside in this world like a fish stuck in a bowl unable to ever
imagine the vastness that dwells outside of its bondage existing
only for the purpose of ones amusement.

Like gamblers we go through life placing our bets some say its luck
but we say its perseverance
if you follow the path that is known
you can never travel to that which is unknown
either you stumble upon gold
or be lost and be all alone.

15)   Emerging Winter.
As the stars disappear from the skies
The morning fog hides the cries
Through it emerges rays of hope
As the horizon fills up with eternal scope

The evenings are engrossed in lores
Sitting around fires escaping the cold
The laws of nature come into efect
As winter emerges gone are the rainy days

Blinded by the white snow
we forget we ever felt low.

PART B-

Chapter 1)Armourgadon.

Dajjal,Mahdi and Isa(AS)
Imam al-Mahdi will be called Muhammed-ibn abdullah
which stands for (Muhammded son of abdullah) like the Prophet (saw)
he will be from the decendents of Prophet muhammed from his
bloodline.The Mahdi means the guided and also the one who will
guides others.
He will reside in the world for years before the coming of
Dajjal(Antichrist) it is said he will be changed by god in one night
to be prepared to face the armies of evil and save the rightous
peaple from dajjal.The world will know of his existence and be aware
about his identity when he will be attacked by a huge army which
will rise from Iraq and Syria and approach him to attack him then

the earth will open up and swallow the whole army and all the
Muslims and believers from other religions will know of his arrival.
Dajjal the Antichrist the general of Iblis the devil the one who is
said to bring upon this world the worst terrors the world has ever
seen he will be a young man one of his eyes will be crooked his hair
will be curly his skin will be reddish he will be short man but very
big built when peaple see him they will say he is huge in size.
He will walk the earth for forty days the first day will be as long
as a year the second day will be as long as a month and the third
day will be as long as a week as most religious texts are revealed
they are understood by different peaple in different ways one way to
understand this revelation is to think about a person who is having
a very bad day they say they had a very long day which means that
when we have a bad time it seems to us that time is passing very
slowly in that way these texts indicate that the first day will be
as long as a year meaning peaple will suffer so tremendously that
one day will seem like a year and so on.
He will be the richest man on earth in a revelation by prophet
Muhammed(saw) it is stated that the earth will dig up its riches for
him.
He will travel around the world in a flying donkey with wings spread
out and in one day he will conquer the world other than Macca and
Madina where he wont be allowed to enter as it will gaurded by the
angels according to another Hadith.
If we try to understand this revelation we must keep in mind that
the prophet was a man in the fifth century Arabia where peaple
travelled on donkeys and horses and the technology we have today
would be considered impossible so he revealed this revelation to the
peaple according to his mindset in that time period but if we as
peaple of modern society look at this hadith we can understand that
he meant an airplane a modern super sonic jets can easily travel
around the world in one day.
Before his coming there will be a year with shortage of rainfall
then the next even reduced rainfall and the third year before his
arrival there will be no rainfall on earth.
When he will travel around the world he will claim to be the prophet
of god the messiah and once he has acquired followers in large
numbers he will tell them i am you lord i am god worship me and none
beside me.To make peaple beleive in him he will perform miracles as
the world will be facing drought and famine he will go to a land and
announce to the peaple beleive in me and i shall pour rain upon your
lands and grow crops upon your feilds and then then rain will come
falling from the skies and the peaple astonished with the miracle
and relieved to be out of there misery will accept him as there lord
and bow down in worship.
As we have been told by the prophet of god dajjal will be a human so
how can a human perform such acts we might ask ourselves but then if
you look modern technology is it anything less than what would have
been considered magic in the past,the American technology known as
HAARP has the capabilities to create artificial rainclouds and
control the weather so we can a man can use modern technology to
decive the peaple and as we know the dajjal means the greatest of
decievers.

Then he will go to a man and say will you beleive in me if i brought
back your parents from the dead and the man will say yes and with
the help of two gin made to look like his parents he will decieve
the man.Again with modern technology such as
plastic surgery and research going on in human and animal cloning
which is getting quite succesful it is very possible to decieve and
we have been told there he will be the greatest of decievers.
As Prophet Muhammed(saw) said There will be no deception greater
than him and never has the world seen terror as will be unleashed
upon the peaple on the coming of the general of the devil.
On his forehead will be written Kafir(disbeliever) that all
beleivers literate and illiterate will be able to read.
He will have fire in one hand and water in one hand and his fire
will be water and water fire so prophet says go and jump in his fire
to be saved just another example of his deceptive nature and the
prophet is indicating here that peaple should do the opposite of
what he says as it will all be an illusion.
A brave man will come to the peaple on that day and tell them he who
claims to be your god is the deciever the dajjal and his followers
will be angry with this man so they will take him to the dajjal and
say lord this man disbelieves in your powers so the dajjal will cut
the man in half and then bring him back to life and he will look at
him with a smile now do you beleive that i am your lord and the man
will look at him and smile back and say now Im assured your not as
my prophet had warned me you will be able to do this once but you
cant repeat yourself and he wont be able to do it,This is from
another authentic Hadith.
As the world will be filled with injustice,crime and sins under the
rule of the deciever Al-Mahdi will take his fellow rightous
companions and hide as he wont have the power to defeat the powers
of Dajjal.
And then the day will arrive as the Mahdi with his small army will
be praying in a mosque, the heavens will answer there prayers as the
skies will split open and from the heavens on the wings of two
angels will arrive the true Messiah the general who will lead the
forces of good against the evil ones Jesus(Isa(AS) he will enter the
mosque he will have a long black beard and long black hair which
will be falling on his shoulders like droplets of water as the
muslims start noticing this man they will realise that the true
Messiah Isa(AS) has arrived Imam Al-Mahdi will walk back and offer
Isa(AS) the position of Imam but the Messiah will reply every nation
has there appointed Imam and you are the Imam of the world for this
appointed time and you are to lead he will stand behind Imam Al-
Mahidi to pray.
As we know Prophethood ended with Prophet Muhammed(saw) as he was
the seal on prophethood so Jesus (Isa(AS) wont return as a prophet
or bring a new revelation he will implement the Quran and lead the
armies of god.
Then Isa(AS) will inform his army about the rewards god has set for
them in the heavens as there souls will leave this world.
Then he leads the army with Al-Mahdi and the rest of the Muslims to
face the armies of Dajjal and in Al-Maqdis the two armies meet in
the Holy lands of Jerusalem.Where Dajjal with his massive army is

ready to destroy the last obstacle to conquer earth and set up the complete rule of his master Iblis.

The two armies meet on the borders of the temple of solomon with the powers of the Gin and the wicked men by his side Dajjal feels confident of his victory over Al-Mahdi unaware that the true Messiah has arrived with the angels and the powers vested to him from the heavens as the battle rages on and the wicked clash with the rightous demons with angels and then in the midst of the intence battle which shakes the whole of earth to its core the eyes of the two generals meet and as the false messiah realises that the true messiah has arrived he tries to run away from the battle feild and is chased down by Isa(AS) and as the dajjal tries to melt away leaving the impression on peaple that he truly was god Isa(AS) strikes him down by the powers vested to him by god and the skies crumble and the earth skakes as the slain Dajjal falls to the ground and the fighting stops and everybody is looking at Isa(AS) as he asks the peaple following him if he truly was god then how did i kill him and the whole battlefeild is silent and frozen like time itself has stopped then everyone bows down to in prostration to the one god All praises to God.

After the great war Al-mahdi will disappear and Isa(AS) will be the caliph of the earth and establish a peaceful rightous rule on earth till he passes away.

Then the heavens will unleash upon earth a soft wind which will take the breathe out of all believers and as there souls leave this realm the quran will be taken from the earth and the kaaba will be destroyed as yajuj and majuj are let free upon manking as they kill and rape and destroy everything in there path a landslide will take place in the east one in the west and one in the Arabian Peninsula and a fire will spread from yemen and a smoke will cover the earth and then beast of earth will released upon mankind a beast soo large and vicious man has never seen before and it will speak human tounge as mankind is wiped out from earth the yajuj and majuj the only ones left they are also humans as there children of adam but they are different then the rest of humanity will turn there weapons on the heavens and attack the heavens and by gods will those weapons will be turned against them and destroy there existance.

Then death will be unleashed upon the Gin and the angels Iblis and his followers will try to run and hide but as none can they shall also face death and so will the angels.

Then death will confront Allah "O allah all those in the heavens and earth have come to an end except for those who you wish to remain and allah will say who remains and the angel of death will reply Jibreel,Mikaeel,and Israfeel and the angels carrying your throne remain then allah(god)will say let death come to them and again allah will ask who remains only you and I and then allah will say I created you for a purpose and now it has come to an end now die death will taste death and then allah will say who remains I am the Almighty allah for who is the devine rule today where are the tyrants and dictators where are the rulers only i remain.And there shall be creation once again as we came before we shall come again. If you look at it from a scientific point of view scientists say the world was created by the big bang from one dot of energy eveything began and its expanding and eventually it will condence back to that

one from which it began so in different words its the same result
one shall return to where one came from.

Chapter 2)Big boss and the grey state.

Big boss is an indian Telivision show produced by Endemol shine
India it was syndicated internationally and extended into seven
languages.
The contestants are called housemates and live in a specially
cnstructed house that is isolated from the outside world.Housemates
are voted out,usually on a weekly basis,until only one remains and
wins the cash prize.During their stay in the house,contestants are
continiously monitered by live television cameras and personal audio
microphones twenty four hours seven days a week.
The icon used for this show while potraying the name is an EYE
depicting an all seeing eye which we all familiar with the
illuminati and the the new world order know to represent a society
which is completely under the control and survalaince of the few
chosen global elites where every human loses there basic forms of
privacy and freedom and is living under a tyranical rule.The first
episode of Big boss premiered on third november 2006 and lasted till
26 january 2007 Around thirteen years have passed and now as im
facing circumstances where my every thought,action and words are
beinge recorded and ditributed across societies it makes me think
about this show and is it another on of the propaganda machines used
by the elites to make us the common peaple accept living life
without our basic freedoms and privacy was this show just used to
subconsciously prepare our minds to accept our upcoming fate of
living in an episode of big boss unwillingly.
A similar living situation is potrayed in the trailer of the film
entitled Gray State depicting the coming of the new world order in
which a family in the USA is shown eating in there house where they
are beinge monitored by a camera and events such as RFID chips
beinge installed inside peaples hands which are beinge used for all
transactions and ways of identification riots are beinge oppressed
by UN military police brutalities and mass holocast where peaple are
shown in a line waiting to be murdered systematicly like the nazis
did to the jews in the satanic events which occurred in world war
two,suprisingly the movie never premiered as the the film maker
crowley twenty nine years of age with his wife and five year old
daughter were murdered in there suburban Apple Valley home south of
Minneapolis the bodies were found after several weeks the house had
multiple cameras and security alarms installed which did not pick
anything up,the case was closed as a suicide even after large scale
protests of his fans claiming they were murdered by the agents of
the New world Order.
With RFID chips beinge installed by the bill and milanda gates
foundation in Africa and brutal riots in America, wars tearing up
most parts of the world and the ongoing corona virus controversy
with the expected economic collaps coming in the aftermath and
facing the impact of modern technology in which
Neuroscientists study the inner workings of the human brain. To do
this, they may listen in as tiny nerve cells, or neurons,
communicate with each other. Their chatter consists of tiny zaps of

electricity. These electrical signals form thoughts and feelings.
They also control the body.
A single neuron fires off a jolt of electricity in response to a
very specific trigger. Scientists call each jolt an action
potential.
For instance, some nerve cells involved in vision fire only when the
human eye sees certain colors. Others fire when the eye detects
basic shapes, or the edges of objects.
Many action potentials combine to form bigger patterns of brain
activity. These patterns become thoughts, movements and more.
Imagine that those vision neurons detect a mix of colors and edges
that look like a baseball, for example. Other networks of neurons
may tell the arm to reach out and pick it up. Still other networks
may form thoughts about playing catch.
These patterns of thought and movement, combine to form brainwaves.
These are overall patterns of the electrical activity happening in
the brain at any one time.
These can be read now by the mobile towers and smartphones speaking
from personal experience which are part of our daily lives which
makes us wander are we already living in a grey state.

Chapter 3)Communism.

Communism is a philosophical, social, political,economic ideology
and movement whose ultimate goal is the establishment of a communist
society,namely a socioeconomic order structured upon the ideas of
common ownership of the means of production and the absence of
social classes,money and the state.
The two classes are the proletariat (the working class), who make up
the majority of the population within society and must work to
survive; and the bourgeoisie (the capitalist class), a small
minority who derives profit from employing the working class through
private ownership of the means of production. According to this
analysis, revolution would put the working class in power and in
turn establish social ownership of the means of production which is
the primary element in the transformation of society towards
communism.The soviet Union was the worlds first nominally communist
state,Which resulted in the cold war a war of ideologies and power
between the Capitalist America and the communist Soviet Union,in
which lots proxy war were fough in Korea,Vietnam,Africa the middle
east between these two sides to influence and implement there
authority and ideology upon the rest of the world.But the true
values of communism were lost and in the name of communism, Leninism
was performed in which a dictorial system of goverment who supported
political represion,genocides,extrajudicial
executions,deportations,killing populations in labour camps and
artificially executed famines were created to kill and decrease the
population.
After the Rothschilds eliminated the Russian royal family in the
conflict known as the first world war Communism was introduced in
Russia and athiesm was spread by the illuminati elite,This is also
mentioned in the plan of the grandmaster of the illuminati Albert
Pike.Some elites use the Idea of communism to implement complete
goverment control over the state and then declare dictatorship.

Chapter 4) Feminism.

Feminism is a range of social movements,political movements and ideologies that aim to define and establish the political,economic,personal and social equality of sexes.Feminism incorporates the position that societies prioritize the male point of view,and that women are treated unjustly within those societies.Efforts to change these inequalities and bring equality between the gender is supposed to be the motive behind the Feminist movement as we know equality and justice are very important factors for the growth and benifit of our female counterparts in society so we understand and respect the values of this movement and that it is neccessary in some parts of our society where male dominance,rape,domestic violence come into play such acts of evil need to be forbidden and men and women together should fight to stop such brutal evil acts.Like the Prophet Muhammed (SAW) said the best of men are the ones who are best to there wife.But this movement is also used by some satanic organisations to spread evil and corruption in society in modern T.V shows like Sex in the city,It is portrayed that women who drink all night,party have casual intercourse are considered modern so acts of evil are getting confused with comitting sins,these shows are made purposely to spread the ideas of adultery,alcohol and all sorts of immoral behaviour in the name of modernity.And some feminists confuse the ideas of sin with equality which are done by certain organisations purposely.Women are objectified by these peaple who use women to attract and promote there ideas,products and busineses.As we have seen revealing clothes are used on women to publisice products by certain organisations.In Europe and America women are protesting by showing there naked bodies in public,nude beaches are a common sight,In the United kingdom you can hire naked women to come clean your house,Feminism and Satanism are two different aspects which our women need to understand for there benifit and security from such evils.Men and women are both required to uphold the basic rules and decencies in our societies to flourish and grow while protecting ourselves from Evil.

Chapter 5) God particle.

God particle AI and other dimentions
The European Organisation for Nuclear Research known as CERN is a European research organisation that operates the largest particle physics laboratory in the world.Established in 1954,the organisation is based in a northwest suburb of Geneva on the Franco-Swiss and has twenty three member states.Israel is the only non-European country granted full membership.CERN is a official United Nations Observer. CERN's main function is to provide the particle accelerators and other infrastructure needed for high energy physics research as a result numerous experiments have been constructed at CERN through international collaborations.The main site at Meyrin hosts a large computing facility,which is primarily used to store and analyse data from experiments as well as simulate events.Researchers need remote access to these facilities so the lab has historically been a major

wide area network hub.CERN is also the birthplace of the world wide
web.
The Large Hadron collider(LHC)is the worlds largest and most
powerful particle accelerator.It first started up on 10 september
2008,and remains the latest addition to CERN's accelerator
complex.The LHC consists of a 27 kilometer ring of superconducting
magnets with a number of accelerating structures to boost the energy
of the particles along the way.Inside the accelerator,two high
energy particle beams travel at close to the speed of light before
they are made to collide.
The Higgs boson is an elementary particle in the Standard Model of
particle Physics,produced by the quantum excitation of the Higgs
field,The higgs boson was initially discovered as a new particle in
2012 based on collisions in the LHC at CERN it is also known as God
particle.
Some theories suggest that the formation of tiny quantum black holes
could generate due to the experiments taking place in the (LHC)
Large Hadron Collider when two particles are colliding with one
another in the speed of light it could result in the formation of
quantum black holes.
Black holes is a region of spacetime where gravity is so strong that
nothing no particle or light can escape from it it sucks everything
inside even time comes to a stop at a black hole,some theories claim
that black holes could be portals as things are sucked inside they
might be coming out somewhere from a white hole the only white hole
we are aware
of is the BIG BANG.
In Quantum Physics scientists have come up with theories of parellel
universes which states that our universe might be one of the many
universes in existance this theory can be related to the verses of
the Quran where God states that he created seven heavens and we
exist at the lowest heaven and only when we die in this world do we
wake up in reality.
There is another theory in Quantum physics called entanglement which
states that when two particles are kept in close contact and there
properties become linked they become entangled and even if you send
one in the opposite direction, one particle could be on the moon and
one on the earth they will still remain entangled no matter the
distance the connection between the particles dosent change and when
heated up one particle can move from one place to another without
travelling in the space or matter in between like teleportation.
It is stated in the Bhagwat geeta that if we take the tip of our
hair and devide it a hundred times and take one part and again
devide it a hundred times thats how small our soul is and it is in
our heart and it is what gives our material body consiousness but
according to the quran our true bodies are not in this world we are
incomplete in this material body and after death our soul leaves
this realm and joins with our true body the eternal body in heaven
or hell or the spirit realm known as Barzakh.So if we think of the
soul as an undiscovered particle in our heart providing consiousness
to our material body it can be understood by the theory of
entanglement that when we die our soul has an entangled particle in
our eternal body so this particle just teleports from this realm to
that realm in our eternal body and we wake up in reality just like

when a child is inside a mothers womb that is there entire world and they have no idea what lies beyond till they come out into the greater reality.
Modern Science is coming up with theories such as the existance of more than three dimentions with einsteins theory of relativity which claims that Time is the fourth dimention and modern scientists proving this theory as it is seen that when an object is travelling close to the speed of light than time slows down inside that object but goes on at the same speed outside of that atmosphere, suppose a space ship was travelling at the speed of light and the person inside sat in the space ship for a few hours but when they will come out of the ship years would have passed in the outside world.
Now modern science is claiming that inside the smallest particles exist strings of energy which keep moving faster than the speed of light and they are what composes and gives shape to the smallest particles such as quarks inside protons and neutrons and the electrons but to prove this theory mathematically scientists needed to consider that there are six to seven dimentions which exist this theory is called string theory which makes scientists believe that there might be whole worlds out there that humans have no idea about.
The intresting thing about this claim is we find in the Quran God has revealed that there are seven heavens into existance and we have been told that there are countless worlds which we have no idea about and will only abide in the afterlife so modern science and revelations are unfolding like two sides of the same coin.
Linda Dalrymple Henderson Art historian at the University of Texas qouted that "how can we be naive enough not to beleive in something we cant see"she is talking about the existance of multiple dimentions isnt that what beleivers are all about believing in what we cant see.
Most of our universe is composed of the unseen which scientists claim exist but they still cant see like the Graviton the quantom particle which makes gravity come into effect most of the universe is composed of dark matter and energy which is made up of particles which are still unseen so coming back to the human soul which is just another particle which is still beyond human understanding.
Artificial Intelligence(AI) is intelligence demonstrated by machines,unlike the natural intelligence displayed by humans and animals.
Leading AI textbooks define the feild as the study of "intelligent agents" any device that perceives its chance of successfully achieveing its goals.
Elon musk stated in an interview artificial intelligence is like summoning a demon into the world.At another interview when asked about the fact that other developers of AI dont show the same level of concern over the dangers of AI Elon Musk replied "Fools" and laughed and stated most AI experts think they know more than they do,most peaple cant accept the idea that a machine can be a lot smarter than them.Dangers of AI are much greater than nuclear war heads destroying the world Tesla claims they are already at the cutting edge of developing a super intelligent AI.Humanity together should make a decision about creating a super intelligent AI but

does all of humanity ever get a say or just the peaple sitting on
top make the call and the rest just obey.
Elon musk claims if a group of peaple manage to create an AI with
god like intellience they could take over the world a human dictator
would eventually die but an AI will be immortal from which we can
never escape.
In the movie the Matrix there was a scene in which it was said-
"Sometimes in the twenty first century all of mankind was united in
celebration we marvelled at our own magnificence to give birth to AI
and it was the doom of mankind"
Now with modern technology it makes us consider the fact that
another science fiction proposition could be closer to coming into
reality.
Googles AI administrator deepmind can learn like humans and is much
smarter and has access to all of googles data it is possible for
this AI to take control of its servers and do whatever it wants.
Scientists claim AI is teaching the machines and the machines are
becoming smart "We dont programme the machines they learn by
themselves" another statement of AI developers.
Now it makes one wander how does an AI teach the machines if we
consider the beginning of technology and calculations which give
birth to theories and the computer language of binary,Maths was not
created by humans it was discovered as it already existed and all
the universe and everything in existance can be defined by numbers
the famous Indian Scientist Aryabhata claimed his discovery of the
number zero came to him at a dream the binary language is made up of
ones and zeroes and is the base for computer languages.All of modern
technology including computers and the internet is dependent on
electricity.In the Quran it is stated that the gin were created by
allah in a smokeless flame which can be recognised as electricity.
The equations of quantum mechanics would develop microscopic
switches that direct the flow of tiny electrons and control everyone
of todays computers,digital cameras and telephones.
With the modern development of quantum computers soon to be coming
into effect it could be possible developing Super artificial
intelligence could be much closer than we expected which will be
much smarter than humans.Now if we consider the facts that gin are
created from electricity and like elon musk says AI is like
summoning a demon it could be considered that AI is nothing other
than the gins beinge pulled out from other dimentions.Elon musks
company Neuralink is working on brainchips which will be implanted
inside the human brain these chips are as small as a coin they are
supposed to help in curing certain illness but the future of this
technology as elon musk claims is to connect the human brain with
the internet so human brains will be directly connected with the
internet and have complete access off all the information availaible
in the internet inside there brains and the memories and thoughts of
humans can be stored using this chip and elon musk claims they can
implement those memories and thoughts inside another humans body or
a machine body so if super intelligent AI are developed and the data
is put in a chip and placed inside a human brain it could be
possible for a AI to control the human mind another theory and which
is more achievable is complete clones of Humans are beinge created
already using AI these are called avatars these could be developed

into machines looking exactly like humans and if super intelligent
AI could be installed into such bodies it would look like a human
with a immortal body and super intelligence.
Now if we consider some of the hadiths by prophet Muhammed(SAW) on
the end of time and dajjal we are told that dajjal already exists
and is in an island and will be released upon mankind in the end of
times so could it be that the dajjals island exists in some other
dimention and as certain scholars claim that the research going on
in cern where particles are collided with each other in the speed of
light which according to scintists could create quantum black holes
or it could be worm holes from which a gin could enter this world so
it is a possibility that dajjal will be a Super intelligent AI in a
machine body looking like a human brought into this world through
some kind of worm hole and as it is said in another hadith he will
go to a man and ask him will you consider me your lord if i bring
back your parents from the dead and the man will say yes and then he
will tell two gin to occupy the bodies of his parents and they will
come stand before the man and he will beleive the dajjal to be god
and if we consider this hadith it is very much possible for modern
technology in the coming future to clone two peaple looking like the
mans parents using machine bodies and as it is said gin will occupy
the bodies artificial intelligence with the thoughts and memories of
his parents could be implanted in the machine bodies so it can be
concluded that in modern science and magic go hand in hand.

Chapter 6)HAARP.

Japan and USA

HAARP(High frequency active Auroral research programme) It is a
technology which can control and manipulate radio frequencies and
natural calamities as well as cause artificial rainstorms. It was
established by America in 1993,Its a feild of research on the
Ionosphere.
The earths atmosphere is devided into many layers from the surface
and extending upto 14.5 kilometers
is the Troposphere then comes the Stratosphere starting just above
the troposphere and extends upto 50 kilometers high then the
Mesosphere,Thermosphere and we arrive at the Ionosphere above that
is the Exosphere the outermost layer.The ionosphere is ionized by
solar radiation,it plays an important role in atmospheric
electricity and forms the inner edge of the magnetosphere,among
other functions it influences radio propagation.Radio propagation is
the behavior of radio waves as they travel or are propagated from
one point to another,or into various parts of the atmosphere.As a
electromagnetic radiation.
It basically means all the telecomunication, internet
services,television which we use are operated by frequencies
travelling to the ionosphere and reflecting back to earth so without
the ionosphere none of this will be possible.
The American research facility was located in Alaska and was under
complete military control they had claimed its purpose was to
understand the causes of natural calamities and changes in
weather.But it is widely believed by many theorists that it can be

used to control and cause natural events such as a rainstorms or natural calamities such as earthquake and Tsunamis.

Russia opposed this research facility claiming the United states was making a weapon which may influence the near earth medium the ionosphere with high frequency radio waves to cause natural disasters.

HAARP is the test run for a super-powerful radiowave beaming technology that lifts areas of the ionosphere by focusing a beam and heating those areas.Electromagnetic waves then bounce back onto the earth and penetrate everything living and dead.
(By Dr.Nick Begich and Jeane Manning,Book Angles dont play with HAARP 1995.)

The HAARP is used to generate beams of frequencies and then they concentrate those beams on a particular position on the inosphere which charges up the particles and these particles and the frequency reflect back on the earth and effect the other layers of atmosphere.

2011 Tohoku earthquake and Tsunami:
Many theorists believe that the earthquake and Tsunami of the pacific coast of Tohoku which devastated eastern Japan was not an natural disaster but a mad made attack using HAARP.
On friday eleventh of march an undersea megathrust earthquake of magnitude (9.0,9.1 Mw) the epicenter approximately seventy kilometer east of the Oshika Peninsula of Tohoka.It swept the Japanese mainland and killed over 15,899 peaple,injured 6157 and 2529 peaple went missing by the last police report. The world banks estimated economic cost was US dollars 235 Billion making it the costliest natural disaster in history,But was it just a natural phenomena or a planned attack by a superpowerfull weapon some theorists claim that it was an attack by the United States of America on Japan using HAARP as they found that before the occurence of the disaster,the ionosphere above the epicentre
of the earthquake was heated up the particles were charged up for three days which might have reflected back on the atmosphere and shocked the earth causing the disaster.
The purpose of Americas attack:-
The second world war had ended with America bombing the Japanese cities Hiroshima and Nagasaki with atomic bombs as Japan surendered it became a client state,America dimilitarised the Japanese military set up Military bases of its on in there lands and had substantial control over the major decisions of the state and had put restrictions on Japan and garunteed to come to Japans aid if Japan was under attack but with the passage of time the Japanese economy boomed and the goverment increased there military capabilities ignoring the US restrictions and in August 2009 with the victory of (DPJ) Democratic Party of Japan and Hatoyama Yokio on a mission to regain the lost japanese pride changes were set upon Japan for the following two years which eventually led to the catostrophic event.The PM started making changes in there foreign policies he wanted to establish equal relations with the US and make japan a soverign nation he wanted to continue the free trade but japan would

be making the active decisions and he wanted to reduce the US
military footprints in Japan as many localities where the US bases
were set up resented the Americans he wanted to reduce and remove
American forces from Japan and create new good relations with the
other Asian countries to lessen there dependencies on America,for
the US these were huge blows as Japan was there main hold to
maintain there power in Asia and the pacific coast losing there hold
on Japan would result in huge economic and military loses for
America reducing there hold on Asia.
AFTER EFFECTS OF THE DISASTER:-
US and Japans Alliance gets stronger under new leadership of PM Noda
Yasuhiko.
In meeting with Barack Obama key changes in Japans foreign policy.
America regains greater control over Yen and its value.
Increase of US forces in Japan.
Relocation of futenme air station to camp schwab.
Trans paific partnership proposed and approved which the previous
goverments had backed away from due to opposition from domestic
agricultural intrests.
Japan agreed with US and south korea to oppose North Korea on the
reopening of six party talks.
Coincidence or pre planned this disaster took Japan back to beinge a
US client State.

Bell Island Canada:-
Peaple claimed they heard weird noises between 1am and 2am
everynight on Bell island few kilometers off the coast of Canada and
while this happened there electrical sockets in there home blew up
so peaple started protesting that the goverment was doing some kind
of testing and the US goverment was blamed.The US goverment declared
those were the sounds of Fighter Jets creating a sonic boom which is
a loud noise that occures when the Jet overcomes the speed of sound.
Residents protested that they have never seen any planes and how
does that explain there electrical sockets blowing up then the
goverment declared that it was thunderstorms and the protests were
shut down many conspiracy theorists beleive that it was just another
incident where HAARP was beinge tested.
On the Illuminati card game we find certain cards which look
surprisingly similar to the disasters in Japan and the capabilities
of HAARP so one may wander is that just another coincidence or are
these pre planned events by the forces of Evil.

Chapter 7)Enoch.

First to call Jihad in the name of Allah,and the first person allah
taught to write.
In the bible his name is Enoch,he was a prophet he was sent upon
humanity to save peaple from zina(Adultery) and violence,he was
elevated to the fourth heaven where his soul was taken by Malik-ul
maut,Allah told the angel of death to take his soul at the fourth
heaven,no one else passed away at that level.Prophet Muhammed(saw)
confirms in sahih Al-Bukhari that when he went for mihraj,he met
Idris (AS),In the fourth heaven after the death of Idris(AS)

corruption increased on earth while the peaple believed in allah and praised him.

After the death of Adam(AS) upto thousand years peaple believed in one lord.Then changes took place shaitan takes the opportunity to whisper to the peaple he greived about the rightoues men who had passed away and said lets put a rock to remember them by the peaple agreed as they still worshipped allah.While shaitan waited patiently he waited for this generation to pass the next generation he told to make human beings out of there rocks shapes of humans,he told them these were your grandfathers they deserved a little more respect than that he let that generation pass,then he went to the next generation and told them you dont know what your forefathers used to do they used to worship these idols,these are statues which brouth them goodness.The younger generations saw these statues and thought these are our gods and they completely forgot about Allah.This was the time prophet   Nur(AS) was sent by god,and the great flood which destroyed mankind.

The Dead sea scrolls

In the year 1946,in the region now known as the West bank,a group of teenagers were playing while they discovered some large clay jars and inside were a series of ancient scrolls, combined they came to be known as the dead sea scrols inside these scrols were a religious text which could paint a picture about true history and what exactly had happened before Noah(pbuh)was sent by god and the world was ruined by the great flood,modern science has proved that there truly was a flood resulted by the melting of the glaciers in the poles which would have created waterfalls as large as two times the world trade centres on cities such as Manhatten,the scroll is about noahs grandfather Enoch the one known as Idris(AS).In the scrols it is mentioned that beings from the heavens known as fallen angels in the bible were sent down on earth they are reffered to as the watchers and they fell for the human women and had intercourse with them and the offsprings that were born were huge in size and very powerful known as the Nephilim,we can understand these were the giants mentioned in ancient lores and all the heavenly books and till the early twentieth century there were bones found all over the world which were huge,bones belonging to giants and were published in newspapers such as newyork times but for some reason we are told today that these are fairy tales this should give peaple a greater idea about there naive mentality of belief and consider things with a more open minded attitude.In it we also find that Enoch was taken to the heavens in a chariot on flames which is also mentioned in the Quran.

In the Sumerian sciptures there are mentioned that a group of beings visited earth called the Annunaki and interbred with humans and created a new species, there are also mentions of genetic modification in human DNA to create these new species which they used to harness gold for them.According to Sumerians the Annunaki are the one who brought advanced technology to the Sumerians in the old world.In the Quran also it is stated that magic began from Babylon an older Sumerian civilisation but the fallen angels are known as djinn(Demons).In modern technology today scientist have developed the technology to change and modify genes of humans so the past coincidies again with the future.In the hindu scriptures as

well we find stories of demigods having children with humans,and the
possibility of advanced technology to be available to the peaple of
the past this would explain some of the structurs such as,The
pyramids which seem impossible to be built at that time in the
thought to be time span,and there are many mystries behind the
pyramids used for harvesting energy in some way,which the famous
scientist Nicola Tesla claimed.In the book of Enoch as well it is
stated the Watchers taught modern technology to humans and this
transformed society drastically and there was a lot of
corruption,fornication,war and disease spread in the land causing
the world to be ended.There is another verse in which Enoch claims
that the lord of the spirits showed him the secrets of lighting and
he wandered if this was a curse or a gift.
In modern times we can have an understanding of this phenomena as
electricity which is also the core of modern technology so the
religious scriptures that most peaple today will say are discussed
by mad men and are fairy tales have certain strong connections
joining the past with the present.

Chapter 8)Illuminati.

Illuminati are generations of satanic bloodlines which have gained
the most power over time or known as satans elite.There are thirteen
families in the world who are known as the royal bloodlines these
are some of the most influential and richest families in the world
controlling the most of the world and its riches without ever coming
out in the open like the puppet masters controlling the show from
behind the scenes never ever coming out in the open.Long ago in the
dark unwritten pages of human history,powerful kings discovered how
they could control other men by torturing,magical
practises,wars,political's,religion and intrest taking.These elite
families designed stratergies and tactics to continue their occult
practises.
In mockery and imitation of gods twelve tribes,satan blessed twelve
bloodlines,one of these bloodlines was the Ishmae bloodline from
which a special elite line developed alchemy,assassination
techniques and other occult practises.One line was
Egyptian/Celtic/Druidic from which druidism was developed.One
bloodline was in the orient and developed oriental magic.One lineage
was from Canaan and the Canaanites.It had the name Astarte, then
Astorga,then Ashdor and finally Astor.
The royalty of the tribe of Dan,the thirteenth or the final
bloodline was copied after gods royal lineage of Jesus.This was the
satanic house of David with there blood which they believe is not
only from the house of David but also from the lineage of Jesus who
they say had a wife and children,and is also merged with the blood
of Lucifer(Iblis)the Gin or the lord of the demons.
One of the bloodlines goes back to Babylon and are descendant from
Nimrod.The mystery religions each had there secret countries which
ruled them and have remained hidden from the history books.

                 The Merovingian Bloodline
This is the thirteenth bloodline which originates from the house of
David and is the bloodline from which the antichrist will come

from,this family can be traced back to ancient Egypt and its routes can be traced to egyptian gods which are the Gin (demons) the eye of horus is in modern times known as the sign of the Illuminati.The British Isles are claimed to to be populated by settlers from ancient Egypt,this bloodline is the only one which can be traced to the ancient times but there is no proof.

The egyptian pyramids are the worlds most mystirious structures with hidden secrets,the golden ratio can be found in the pyramids,Nicola Tesla the great scientist was obsessed with the structure and said they served a higher purpose and the secrets of unlimited energy where hidden in those structures,In the book of Enoch there are mentions of superior beings called the Annunaki,who made the humans there slaves to harness energy and gold and were the creators of the Pyramids,These Annunaki are what, i believe to be the Gin race,We learn that the Illuminati are the ones who control the prices of gold and one of there main goals is to harvest all the gold in the world,One of the major scandals of the Paper Currency system is to give paper in exchange for gold,It is a deceptive plan and can be understood as one of the greatest Scams pulled in human history by the few who want control over the many all.This world is like a fish tank and we are the fish swimming inside a small carier and thinking this is all there is in existance spending our lives never even considering the fact that there exists things beyond our imagination in this world and in the heavenly worlds but we go through our lives without ever even considering these issues thats exactly what these elites and satan worshippers want to enslave the human race they must take away the freedom of the minds then they will attack us physically.The Prophet Qouted that in the end times the war will be of ideologies and the devil weapon will be deception there is a qoute that the greatest trick the Devil ever pulled was that he dosent exist.

Further we have details about the rest of the families involved and associated with the Illuminati keep reading.

Astor family

Astor original founder of the Astor fortune was John Jacob Astor (1763-1884),John Jacob Astor was born in walldorf,Germany from a jewish bloodline.From England to America he travelled and the story goes he came to America penniless and that maybe true but he soon joined the Masonic lodge and in two, three years became the master of the hallond lodge No.8 in N.Y city.

Many of the members of this lodge have good connections to the Illuminati elite.

John Jacob Astor was a cold hearted anti social man
he rose very high in free masonry,The initial financial break came by carrying out a series of shady and crooked real estate deads in the N.Y city area.The next break came when two men known to have been in the Illuminati gave John Jacob Astor a special goverment privilege.The US goverment had placed an emargo on all U.S ships sailing with goods in 1807,But Astor got special permision from these men and made around 2000,000 profit in that days money.He also profited from the civil war in America,The British intelligence worked for the committee of three hundred and for the thirteen top families.The American and british Intelligence have intimate relations with the thirteen illuminati families.He made a monopoly

in the fur trade of the new world all the competition disappeared
how did that happen only he knows.It is said his occult powers could
have been the reason his wife was also from a satanist family,he had
good relations with the politicians of that day.He made a fortune
running Opium to China,the British didnt allow the selling of the
drug Opium in there own states so as they sold it at there colony
China at that time to make the chinese addicted destroy the peaple
and make huge profits at the same time,he owned huge amounts of real
estaet in Newyork city.He sat on the board of directors for the
United states bank which at the time had five directors.They owned
1/20 of Newyork real estate,He owned a large stock of the United
states Bank.They choose to remain in the background not even beinge
on the board of directors of the corporations they owned so there is
no way of knowing how much they actually control most of them left
to England,They are worth forty billion in todays date but there is
no way of knowing how much they have which is concealed from the
public eye.Vincent Astor was a member of forty one private clubs and
was in numerous business which shows just how much power one of
these Astor family members have-
Dir-American Express company
Dir-Atlantic fruit and suger company
Dir-Chase Manhattan Bank of the rockfellers
Dir-City and suburban homes CO
Dir-Classical Cinemotograph corporation
Dir-Cuban-Dominican suger CO
Dir-Great Northern railroad
Dir-Central rail road
Dir-Inter Mercantile Marine CO
Dir-National Park Bank of NY
Dir-NY country trust CO
Dir-weekly publications Inc
Dir-Western Union Telegraph trustee NY
Zoological soc advisor to Bankers trust of NY members Amer Museuam
of Nat.Hist,member not insit of soc,Science (notice these last two
like so many elite controlled organisations are heavily involved in
the spread of the evolution theory.
Berry Smith of Australia wrote in his book final notice there are
thirteen families or groups heading up the world goverment
plan.These families are found as the thirteen layers of blocks found
on the strange seal on the reserve side of the U.S one dollar
bill.They are also invested in the drug trade destroying humanity
for profit.Astors,Bundys,Du ponts,Freemans Kennedys,Lis,Rockfellers
and Russels nine of the thirteen Illuminati families are invilved in
the drug trade.In the netflix series Narcos it is shown that the CIA
and FBI dont want to stop the drug trade they just to control it and
have the cartels under there control the families have intimate
relations with the CIA and FBI.
Families allied with the illuminati-
Some families work on a business level with the illuminati like the
Mafia families who dont beleive in the occult system but do
understand money and power.Some families are just dragged into this
corrupted world system.Such as the King of Nepal,The British have
done a great job in making Nepal dependent on them Nepal was given
British Education and there leading tribe of warriors have been

serving as British regiment.If the king of Nepal dosent agree with
the NWO they could create a revolution or invasion,They could
arrange the India congress party to invade Nepal,The British MI 6
and American CIA have agents placed over there.
Switzerland has been in the complete control of the Illuminati for
centuries so there is no need for invasion or interference over
there,It can be seen that the shady banking system the swiss banks
and the Hadron Collider which Stephen Hawkings said could bring
large scale destruction on the planet.
Some Scholars claim that the research going on over there could open
a portal to another dimention or a worm hole,this is supported by
Islamic scholars in confirming these other dimentions could be
opening the gateways of the Barzakh the spirit realm or a gateway to
the world of the Gin Race (Demons) the Gin are a different species
residing in another dimension and are also present in this world.
The families in control of the Venice,Switzerland go back to and
have lineages going back to the Byzantine Empire also known as the
Eastern Roman Empire.The powerful families who are not alligned with
the Illuminati are destroyed an example would be the Howard Hughes.
Another example how the Rothschilds destroyed the Romanovs,the
Russian Imperial family which was also an occult bloodline so they
took children as breeders from the lineage secretly to keep the
bloodline alive.The conflicts between these families are also what
is known as the first world war so here is an example of much
influence just a few families of the world hold over the rest of
society.Albert pike also known as the grand master of the Illuminati
had forged a plan for establishing an one world goverment controlled
by the heads of the thirteen families in this plan which was
released by an reporter who got hold of a letter he wasnt supposed
to posess and after printing it he was branded as crazy and
disappeared but the information was out for the few who were willing
to look at the true realities of the world we abide in.

The letter(1871)

The First world war must be brought about in order to permit the
illuminati to overthrow the power of the Czars in Russia and of
making that country a fortress of atheistic communism.The
divergences caused by the agents of the illuminati between the
British and Germanic Empires will be used to foment this war.At the
end of the war,communism will be built and used in order to destroy
the other goverments and in order to weaken the religions.

The second world war must be fomented by taking advantage of the
differences between the fascists and the political zionists.This war
must be brought about so that Nazism is destroyed and that the
political zionism be strong enough to institute a sovereign state of
Israel in Palestine.During the second world war,International
Communism must become strong enough in order to balance
christendom,which would be then restrained and held in check until
the time when we would need it for the final social cataclysm.

The third world war must be fomented by taking advantage of the
differences caused by the agents of the illuminati between the
political zionists and the leaders of the Islamic world.The war must
be conducted in such a way that Islam and political Zionism mutually

destroy each other.Meanwhile the other nations,once more devided on
this issue will be constrained to fight to the point of
complete,physical,moral,spiritual and economic exhaustion.

Then everywhere,the citizens,obliged to defend themselves against
the world minority of revolutionaries,will exterminate those
destroyers of civilization,and the multitude,disillusioned with
christanity,whose deistic spirits will from that moment be without
compass or direction,anxious for an ideal,but without knowing where
to render its adoration,will recieve the true light through the
universal manifestation of the pure doctrine of Lucifer,bought
finally out in the public view.

This manifestation will result from the general reactionary movement
which will follow the destruction of christianity and atheism both
conquered and exterminated at the same time.
The illuminati have also made connections into the Islamic world
with some of the influential Arabic families such as Sirdar Ikbal
ali shah who has written more than seventy books on Magic and
occultism.
                    The Bundy bloodline
Ted Bundy a serial killer in 1980 America killed countless peaple
and told hif girlfreind the force had made him commit the
murders.After getting arrested in Florida,he would say the power
used to consume him and so he did it.The force was an term used by
satanists to describe the powers they beleive in and claim it can be
used to do good and evil.Suprisingly it is also used in the Movie
star wars this is to make the conspiracy an open conspiracy to
prepare peaples mindset through movies to accept the evil without
even realising what is happening at times,and the true goals of
forming the one world goverment(Agenda 21) is also portayed in
different ways by hollywood to form a greater acceptance of the idea
among the peaple, as we have seen America is always shown as the
country taking charge and saving the world from all evils in
hollywood movies these are just beautiful methods used by the
Illuminati planners to spread there ideology hollywood and the music
industry is controlled by them.Ted bundy was a big fan of rockfeller
and was on a political path till he blew it but there is no way of
knowing if he was connected to the satanists or if he had relations
with the royal Bundy bloodline.
The original Bundy family came to the new world before 1635 to
Boston,most Americans wouldnt consider the Bundies influential but
two Bundy brothers were in control of feeding information to US
president Kennedy and Johnson administration,both Bundy brothers
were involved in the skull and bones.There are countless other
members holding key positions in the US.
                    The Collins
Another Illuminati family with very little public knowledge they
hide there tracks very well.The following is a description of a
highly secret high level satanic meeting,It comes from an ex-insider
who is now a christian,this experience dates to 1955,this is a
meeting held twice yearly to which the rothchilds and the other
families attend,This meeting was in a big room and the grandmother
was a Collins,The Collins family were kept out of the limelight as

they had more occult power than the Rothschild and Rockfellers to make money they do financial work such as exchange money.
The grandmother collins was dressed in black she sat on a gold and ebony moon shaped throne,Behind her sat the grand council with thirteen members,In 1955 it was all males and in 1978 there were several women in it.Gold bars were laid at her feet with lots of jewelery,two boys sat beside her taken to be her sons one of whom was Tom Collins who was later gunned down by the Illuminati.
A great lot of discussions were made of what happened in the last six months to bring the world closer to satans one world goverment,The ark of covenant was discussed and where in Africa it was hidden.Seven children in white were brought in from satanic families and presented before grandmother collins,They laid in prostration to worship her,she would move her scepter with a snake up and down striking the floor to show approval of a child candidate then seven other children were sacrificed for the approved seven children,one for each child whose name will be written by a quill using the sacrificed childs blood.The children were given oaths,The grandmother rotated her chair and announced these are the generation of the future.
The leading satanists feel they have royal blood,the top ones feel they are gods,Tom Collins was in the illuminati but changed heart and started informing the churches what is going on.Tom Collins was then gunned down in a parking lot.
The Du Ponts
They are another satanic royalty,they have been known to marry with other satanic bloodlines among those peaple satanic blood is very important they believe if they have it they can rise to the top.
They have a better hold of the press coverage Britain then the British royal family.
The royalty in Denmark and the British royal family have openly submitted into masonry especially Prince Charles.
Not much is known about them but they are worth billions so hiding there secrets is easy.
The Du points is also one of the richest illuminati families since they made there riches in the gunpowder business in the nineteenth century.
They expanded there wealth through chemical industry and automative Industry.
At one point they were the worlds largest manufacturers of gun powder,the biographies of the Du pont family usually begin with the marriage of Samuel Du pont to Anne Cane from an ancient noble family that lived in Burgandy.It is possible annies bloodline gave the Du ponts there occult powers as she might be tied to the house of David.
At the the time of the marriage Duc d'Orleans grand master of the Grand Orient of France,that is head of all the French masons.
Eluthere Irene Du pont was a director of United States Bank just like Astor.
The freeman bloodline
The amazing thing about this family is that it is not a family that peaple would have thought of as one of the top thirteen families.Stephen M.Freeman runs the legal affairs department of the civil rights division of the anti defamition leugue.The Illuminati

drug money funds this organisation,It is a international Jewish non-goverment organisation based in the United states.ADL states its goal is a dual one to stop the defamation of the Jewish peaple,They claim there ultimate goal is to create a world with no hate or discrimination.But the reality might be different it could be a social organisation which cleans up the drug money of the Illuminati by showing it as donations and parts of that money is used to fund there real goals of spreading satanic ideology of the one world goverment,this example takes us back to the Hadith of Prophet Muhammed (SAW) where he says in the time of dajjal everything will be a deception.Dajjal will come holding heaven in one hand and hell in one hand the prophet says jump into the fire as it will be heaven and his heaven will be hell,this gives the messege that what will be thought as good in the end times will be bad and the bad will be good it will be a world of illusions and dilusions.
To be a researcher and to be informed that the Kennedy family is a top 13 llluminati family is akin to
being told a needle is in a haystack
The origines of the kennedys are from Ireland they were royal families and in power in the sixteenth century there is a branch of the Kennedys in Scotland as well and they are related by inter marriages.
It is clear that there have been quite a number of powerful aristocratic Kennedys. One of the more
powerful recent Scottish aristocrat Kennedys was the Marquess of Ailsa (1872-1943). Because he is
often called the Marquess of Ailsa you might not know him by his name Archibald Kennedy, who was
the 15th Earl of Cassillis. This branch of the Kennedys married into Scottish royalty. For instance, Sir
James Kennedy married Mary, a daughter of King Robert III, and their son was Sir Gilbert Kennedy
was made Lord Kennedy before 1458. Archibald Kennedy was an extremely powerful Freemason and
held numerous key positions in the Grand Lodge of Scotland. He was 1st Grand Principle from 1913
3
to his death in 1943. At his death his titles passed to his brother Charles. Archibald Kennedy was
initiated in Holyrood House Lodge No. 44, Edinburgh, Nov. 17, 1896. William Jessy kennedy 3 another aristrocat was the owner of the ford theatre in which the elites killed president Lincoln.
If John F. Kennedy had not been assassinated and so much about his life examined and written about,
a window allowing us to see the Kennedy Illuminati family may never have opened so wide. First, the
assassination attracted attention. In recent years, the Illuminati have given permission to publishing
houses to print exposes of J.F.K.'s sexual life, etc.11 It is believed that this permission was given in an
effort to deflect criticism of his assassination by allowing his reputation to be tarnished.12 (I hope my
readers are beginning to realize that things are totally corrupt at the top, and that JFK was no different

than so many others that have been and are today at the top of the
political mess in this nation.) John
F. Kennedy had a very active sex life, even after he married Jackie,
and even after he was President in
the White House. For those who don't think secrets can be kept by
the elite, one only has to look at
how John F. Kennedy was able to have sex with many women while
President and to have frequent
nude swim parties at the White House pool and the general public not
know anything about it.13 John
F. Kennedy's lust for women was well known by the elite. Illuminatus
McGeorge Bundy warned his
friend JFK (while JFK was a Senator) that John's openness with women
might get him into trouble
with the public. John F. Kennedy was so open about his sexual habit,
that at one party at the
Mayflower Hotel in Washington, D.C. John F. Kennedy openly had sex
with one pardner in front of
the party, while his friend Senator Estes Kefauver did the same.
Then they swapped pardners and
began again in plain view. John F. Kennedy had many "one-night-
stands" as the world calls them.
These were merely women hustled up by his aides or the secret
service or his friends like Frank
Sinatra. But Kennedy also had long term relationships with some of
the women he was sexually active
with. It is those relationships which reveal so much about the
hidden Satanic side of the KennedYs.

A poem by one of the women associated with Kennedy.
"He would find love
He would never find peace
For he must go seeking
The Golden Fleece."

Joseph Kennedy was the father of John F.kennedy and was known to
have close connections with the Mafia as we learned before the
Mafia(Cosa Nostra) have close connections with the Illuminati as
they perfomed murders and controlled trade unions and most of the
dirty work required by these elites.
It is a theory that John F.Kennedy and the CIA was working with the
Mafia bosses to win the presidential elections but after winning as
he did not return the favours for the Mafia they had him killed.
 As might be expected of any "good" Illuminati family, the Kennedy.
 are
connected to drugs, to the Monarch program, to "death" euthanasia
programs, to the British monarchy,
and to the various organized crimes group., mafias etc
These peaple have hospitals in england and other places in the world
where the elite families give patients drugs which alter with the
minds of the indivisuals at times mixed with cocaine,heroine,alcohol
and other substances till the patients die,they view this practise
to be conducting favours upon humanity by getting rid of the
unwanted peaple according to them,As it is seen in the modern times

elites openly support depopulation so that the rest of society will
have better lives according to them so it is safe to assume ones
they accomplish there one world goverment the world is going to see
terrors unimaginable by human society in the past.

The Li Family

In recent history three Li's stand out as giants.
· The billionaire and de facto ruler of Hong Kong Li Ka-shing.
· Li Peng the ruler of Red China.
· Lee Kuan Yew President (& dictator) of Singapore
These peaple are worth billions and are major players in the coming
of the new world order,the rockfellers and rothschilds have a huge
respect for the chinese and the Japanese compared to other
peaple.These families own political unions,real estates,Banks,Media
and most other resources of the land.
Triad rituals were an elaborate affair but have continued to be
streamlined over the years. The ritual
initiation drew from 3 religious sources: Taoism (magic), Buddhism,
and what might be called
Confucianism. Taoism emphasized the importance of blood ancestry, of
magic, and alchemy. The
traditional initiation lasts about eight hours, and includes ritual
dance, secret hand-shakes, a blood
sacrifice, and pricking the finger of the new initiates.
The Triads have an extremely long history and a lot of heritage. In
order to try to capsulize what they
are one has to look at what they are doing at a particular moment.
At times they are secret fraternity
like the Masons, at other times they have more of the appearance of
a revolutionary army, and at
other times they look like the Mafia. They are all these things. And
so they are a much more complex
group to understand than some of the other secret societies that
might fit into some nice label.
Sometimes their services as hit men are hired out to others. Their
heritage and history make them
almost a sub-culture, and a sub-culture that is difficult for law
enforcement agencies to penetrate.
Their blood oaths and traditions bind them together.
The triads are the worlds most dangerous criminal organisations and
the peaple hardly have any knowledge of them they work for the
illuminati kings and are involved in murder,drugs ect.
The Japanese yakuza the criminal organisation could have ties with
these groups.
The Triads are an occult fraternity which has developed into a major
international organized crime society. It has many agreements with
various families of the Illuminati, and works with them. The Li
family is taking a big role somewhere with the Triads.

The Onassis Bloodline

Aristotle Socrates Onassis -- named after two greek philosophers,
went from being totally broke at
age 21 to being a millionaire at age 23. His father's first name was
Socrates. Aristotle was an
Illuminati king, a shipping tycoon, an intelligent ruthless hard-
driving man, a man of the world who

spoke a number of languages such as French, Spanish, English, Italian, and Turkish. He married
JFK's widow. His everpresent sunglasses made him look like Al Capone to a number of people.
Jackie Bouvier Kennedy Onassis-Her father was a member of the Society of the Cincinnati, the
American equivalent to the Order of the Garter. Her father " Black Jack" was corrupt, what is known
as a womanizer. He worked at making a living from the stock market. Jackie's "step-father" was the
Auchincloss family, an elite family. Her step-father's second wife before Jackie's mother was Senator
Thomas Gore's daughter. Her step-father was in Naval Intelligence. Jackie went to the schools that
the children of the elite go to. On the anniversary of JFK's assassination, Orville & Jane Freeman
were the only ones to remember the date to say or do something about it. Jackie went that day to
Central Park and had a good cry.
He was one of the richest peaple in the world,from a tobaco trader to a shiping owner in world war two he owned the Monte Carlo Casino and made a deal with Saudi Arabia to cunduct Whaling expeditions.

Rockfeller
The Rockefellers were Marrano Jews. The original Rockefeller made his money selling narcotics, (they weren't illegal then). After acquiring a little capital he branched out
in oil. But it was the Rothschild capital that made the Rockefeller's so powerful. "They also financed
the activities of Edward Harriman (railroads) and Andrew Carnegie Steel.
How Rockefeller Found Big Pharma AND Waged War On Natural Cures

It has been said that the Rockefeller family has affected modern society to a degree but what most do not realize is just how much they have made an impact. The family name has now been linked to the suppression of naturalmedicine to found big pharmaceutical companies and make big money.

The West Has the Best and Most Profitable Healthcare in the World

The west is home to some of the best healthcare in the world. Anyone in an emergency which needs prompt medical treatment is better off than those living elsewhere. In the west, people receive healthcare that is much better than what is offered in an establishing nation. However, it is often overlooked that healthcare is now a multi-trillion dollar industry in the west.

The mainstream medicine of today is based on treating people who are ill with drugs, radiation, and operations that are very pricey. What many people do not realize is that the Rockefeller family was the first to recognize the opportunity to take full advantage of what has become an ecosystem with huge profits.

Anyone Questioning Big Pharma Is Branded a Quack and Conspiracy Theorist
Today we live in a world of social media censorship, and anyone who even dares to question the intentions of any of the big pharmaceutical companies is branded insane and given the label of a crazed conspiracytheorist. Any information brought forward about recovery residential or commercial properties of holistic practices and plants that cannot be patented are branded phony news as they are considered to threats to the drugs of the big pharmaceutical companies.

John D. Rockefeller realized the opportunity first. He was an oil mogul who was the first person in the USA to become a billionaire. By the start of the 20th century, he had 90% control over oil refineries in the US with his company Standard Oil. In 1900, researchers came across petrochemicals, and they found out that it was possible to make many chemicals out of oil. The first plastic, which was Bakelite, was made in 1907 from oil.

This meant that Rockefeller had to get rid of what was significant competition. He made use of a strategy that was time-proven, problem-reaction-solution. The concept works when developing an issue that would bring terror to people and then offer them a solution that was pre-planned. He got the help of Andrew Carnegie; he had made lots of money monopolizing the steel industry. The Carnegie Foundation sent Abraham Flexner on a trip around the nation, and he was given the task of reporting the status of medical facilities along with the medical colleges in the United States. This led to the Flexner Report, and this eventually led to modern medication of today.

Cures for Illnesses Such As Cancer Would Be Bad For Business
100 years later and medical colleges produce doctors who do not know anything about holistic practices or the many benefits that herbs have to offer. The government in the United States invests 15% of the Gross domestic item in mainstream health care. This is a system focusing on symptoms, and it produces a flurry of repeat paying clients that is never-ending.

Despite much advancement in medicine, there is still no cure for cancer, diabetes, autism, asthma or even the common cold. Cures for any of these illnesses would only be bad for business. John D. Rockefeller was even behind the establishment of the American Cancer Society in 1913.

Rothschild
The Rothschild family is a wealthy Jewish family originally from Frankfurt that rose to prominence with Mayer Armschel Rothschild (1744-1812),a court factor to the German landgraves of Hesse-Kassel in the Free city of Frankfurt,Holy Roman Empire who established his banking business in the 1760s,

Unlike most previous court factors, Rothschild managed to bequeath
his wealth and established an international banking family through
his five sons,[3] who established businesses in London, Paris,
Frankfurt, Vienna, and Naples. The family was elevated to noble rank
in the Holy Roman Empire and the United Kingdom.During the
nineteenth century the rothschild family owned the largest private
fortune in the world.These are the peaple who set the prices of gold
everyday and control the reserve bank of America.On the back of the
one dollar bill we find a pyramid which is a symbolism of there
organisation the illuminati.These peaple are worth hundreds of
billions and most of there wealth and property are hidden from the
public eye,these are the major players who want to colonise the
world once more and create the new world order in which there
Messiah the Dajjal (antichrist)will take the throne this plan is
also known as the Agenda twenty one which they believe they will
acclomplish by the year 2050.

The Russel Bloodline

They are a scotish originated Aristocratic bloodline holding
influence in England and in American politics they are also involved
in the occults and satanism,these peaple have taken oaths of silence
or death so information is not available about them but this family
are the key players in the satanic rituals,and it is said they are
the family responsible for creating the Skull and Bones
of which George Bush was a member,they also created many other
smaller satanic organisations spreading there ideas around the
world.

Van Dyun bloodline

They were pirates and influencers of witchcraft they played a major
role in satanism in Neatherlands in the old days and were involved
in setting up the Bank of Englan.This family plays a major role in
creating diseases such as the black death in Europe,AIDS and viruses
such as Ebola these are created to lower the population they sit on
the cures till they they are exposed and then sell vacines and
medicines for huge profits this has become one of the major
stratergies of the illuminati to kill the population than come to
public eyes as the saviours and make money out of the cure.The
colonisers of America distributed blankets infected with small pox
to the native Americans and killed millions by disease such dirty
evil methods are the norms followed by these families, this family
is also worth billions but we dont know much about them as there
very secretive.

Chapter 9)Iran.

Party of the
Century &
Leaders
putting up an
Act
(24.08.20)

Just watched a video of Irans 2,500 year celebration of the persian
Empire officially known as the foundation of the Imperial state of
Iran.

It was organised by Mohammad Reza Pahlavi the last shah (king) of Iran.It consisted of an elaborate set of festivities that took place on 12-16 October 1971 it was an event which was seen as the party of the century as the shah spent millions of dollars organising the party calling all the elites of the world in one place Kings and queens,prince and princesses,Prime ministers and Presidents, the elite businessmen all gathered in the middle of the transformed desert into a lavish hangout for the elite,at this time Iran was facing great difficulties as the economy was collapsing peaple were in distress protests were going on, the country was in need for there leader to step up and make some reforms to stabalise the situation and help the peaple he ruled over instead he chose to spend an average estimate of 20 million dollars to throw a party and show off to the world his wealth and status, just another example of how much the elites that rule over us care about the common peaple.This led to a series of events which eventually led to the downfall of the shah by the Iranian revolution of 1979 and sayyid Ruhollah Khomeini came to power to form the Islamic Republic of Iran and ended the 2500 year old Persian dynasty starting from Cyrus the great founder of the Achaemenid Empire,the first persian Empire.The irony was that shah was celebrating the beginning of the monarchy which led to the fall of the monarchy.These events kind of made me think about whats going on in India these days as our ruling BJP goverment and the current prime minister Narendra modis actions, India has the second largest population in the world of 1.3 billion peaple with 6 crore 50 lakh peaple living in poverty and our prime minister is making statues such as the staute of unity which cost 2,989 crores to build compared to the second tallest statue of the world the spring temple budha estimated around 500 crores with such a huge difference in the expenditure of the two projects we might assume its atleast the double in size but no its 29 metres taller so why did it cost 6 times more is it made up of gold ?Thats a question our respected prime minister must answer, other projects such as making a wall to hide the poor peaple of the country and destroying there homes as the president of America Donald trump was coming to visit really makes us wander what happened to the guy claiming to be a peaples leader who called himself fakeer(someone who rejects worldly possesions)and would boost up the economy and remove poverty.These events show us how insignificant the common peaple are for the elites that rule over us and control most of our lives indirectly and are trying to have complete control over us in the future with the coming of the new world order.

Chapter 10)Islamic prophecies.

The prophet Muhammad (saw) had made many prophecies that cant be explained in any other way then he recieved the revalations from the Almighty the creator of the worlds God himself. Most of these were signs of events that will occure when the world will be closing in on the day of Judgement.
As we read in the first revalation that our prophet recieved that made the devil come down in tears
Surah Al-fatihah -

(Alhumdullila hii rabbil aalameen)
"All praises to god lord of the worlds"

(Ar rahman nir raheem)
"The most merciful the entirely merciful"

(Maliki Yauw mid deen)
"Sovereign on the day of judgement"

ARAB BEDOUINS PROPHECY:
A man came to prophet muhammaded and asked him
"Now,tell me of The last hour"
The prophet replied "you will see barefoot,unclothed Bedowins
competing in the construction of tall buildings."
The bedouins were nomads they travelled through the vast deserts and
were constantly on the move even during the Golden Age of Islam when
Arabs were the richest and most learned peaple on earth the bedouins
remained in the same state they had been in for thousands of years
poor,uneducated and cut off from the rest of the world yet the
prophet foretold when the last hour will be upon the world these
peaple will be competing with each other in the construction of the
worlds tallest buildings larger than the mountains which would have
been thought to be impossible at that time but is happening now as
we see the bedouins competing not just with each other but with the
rest of the world.
The prophet also stated that "the hour will not be established until
mountains are moved from there places" as we see in Mecca the
prophets place of birth large mountains have been demolished to
build some tall buildings such as the famous clock tower of Mecca
the third tallest building in the world the idea of demolishing
entire mountains were also thought to be impossible at that time and
is only possible with the advancements in technology in the
twentieth century such as explosives.
The question must arise in ones mind how did these nomads wandering
in the deserts become the richest peaple on the planet it happened
as the earth offered up its riches to them the bedouins struck oil
in the empty deserts they had been wandering
around for years which is one of the most valuable resource in the
world for the last century.
Spread of sexual immorality and disease:
The prophet said the day of judgement wont be upon us until sexual
immorality will have become so common that peaple will be
fornicating in public places like donkeys as we see with modernity
and westernisation having sexual encounters with multiple partners
is thought as a common act.In many holywood movies and TV serieses
we see that they are conveying messeges such as college is a place
where you try out new things which is referred to drugs and multiple
sexual encounters and most movies peaple who get married with the
only woman they have slept with are considered old fashioned it
makes us wander what kind of messege are these film industries
sending to the world.
In europe and America nude beaches and rallies are common findings
as well as public sexual acts.

In UK you can hire a naked maid to come clean your house Peaple even swap there wifes in the name of having fun pornography and sexual acts in media have become common so it is safe to say that even this prophecy is coming true.

He also stated "Never does sexual perversion become widespread and publicly known in certain places without them beinge overtaken by disease that never happened to there ancestors who came before them" As we see diseases such as AIDS which were unheard of before have come to light due to the spread of sexual immorality as the prophet muhammed (SAW)had warned.

World Drowned in Intrest:

The prophet stated "A time will come upon mankind when they will consume intrest whoever does not will be afflicted by its dust" By Islamic law taking intrest is forbidden but as we see today the Islamic countries and the Non-Muslims are completely dependent on central banks and loans with high rates of intrest and credit cards even if not directly indirectly the whole modern world is centered around the system of intrest which came into beinge due to the system of paper currency which is a recent event as in our prophets time finance was based on commodities with intrinsic value such as gold and silver.

The defeat of Rome and conquest of Persia:

During the Battle of the Trench,also known as the Battle of the confederates was a fortnight long siege of Yathrib (now Medina)by Arab and Jewish tribes.The strenght of the confederate armies is estimated around 10,000 men with six hundred horses and some camels,while Medinan defenders numbered 3,000 where the prophet and his followers were under seige beinge outnumbered three to one stairing at certain defeat when the messenger of Allah made some bold predictions he said

(Allah huu akbar-God is most great)"God is most great I have been given the keys of Syria By God I can see its red palaces at the moment,God is most great I have been given Persia,God is most great I have been given Yemen, at that moment the the prophet of god claimed that the muslims will not only take the lands of Yemen and Syria much of which was under the mighty Roman Empire but also that they will defeat the mighty Persian Empire.

Historically muhammeds companions saw this prophecy fulfilled before there eyes as they went on to defeat the romans and conquer Persia.What are the odds that the Muslims who lacked economic and military strenght could topple the superpowers of the world in such a short span of time and captured the world at surprise.

Historian Barnaby Rogerson explains "You have to remember that the two great superpowers of the time The Byzantine Empire(The eastern Roman empire)and Sassanid Persia if your putting it in a modern parlance its like the Eskimos (members of an indigenous peaple inhabiting northern Canada,Alaska and eastern siberia traditionally living by hunting seals and other artic animals) defeating USA and Russia which would be thought of as impossible and nobody can explained how the muslims did in such a short span of time it can only be explained as Gods will.

Prevalence of writing:

A lot of peaple today take for granted the ability to read and write in the past times due to the scarcity of books and teachers not many

peaple were literate it is estimated that the number of peaple that
could read and write in the prophets locality in western saudi
Arabia were around 17 Muhammed(peace be upon him)himself could not
read or write.
He made a prediction that litracy would widely spread in the end
times,He said "Ahead of the hour,the pen will prevail" the arabic
word for pen used here is QALAM which has a wider meaning of
writing.In the modern world literacy is widespread with abundance of
books and magazines which only became possible in the fifteenth
century technological advancements such as printing eight hundred
years after the death of the prophet.
The greening of the Arabian deserts:
The prophet of God foretold that the "The hour will not begin until
the land of the Arabs once again becomes meadows and rivers" this
narration is talking about the deserts of Arabia beinge filled with
greenery as recently as 1986 there little to no farming in these
areas but in the last thirty years it has filled with greenery due
to modern techniques such as centre pivot irrigation(A method of
crop irrigation in which equipment rotates around a pivot and crops
are watered with sprinklers) using waters from deep underground some
which date back to the last Ice age.This prophecy also claimed about
the ancient past as the Prophet of god says once again claiming once
these deserts were filled with vegetation and life,geologists now
claim that once the Arabian penunsila was filled with vegetation by
archeological findings.
The rapid spread and the decline of the muslims:
The prophet of god predicted that Islam will spread East and West,he
said "God folded the earth for me and i saw its east and west and
the dominion of my nation will reach as far as the earth was folded
for me"History bears witness that Islam spread both East and West in
the likeness of which the world had never seen before but the
prophet(saw) also predicted the downfall he said "The nations will
call each other and set upon you,just as diners set upon food."
Someone then asked "Will it be because of our small numbers ?"The
prophet of god replied "Rather,on that day you will be many but you
will be like foam,like the foam on the river" He prophecised that
the muslims will be large in numbers but due to there weakness will
fall, this situation can be described by the radical events that
took place in the Muslim world in the nineteenth and twentieth
century prior to this the muslims were
economically,politically,technologically far ahead of the rest of
the world till all the muslim lands were captured by non-muslim
countries the european powers almost all the fifty muslim countries
existing today were subject to colonial powers at that time there
were around 200 million muslims and today there are around 2 billion
around the world as the prophet of god had predicted that "This
matter will certainly reach every place touched by night and day God
will not leave a house or residence except that God will cause this
religion to enter it".
The name Muhammad means "The praised one",The quran states that how
Muhammads rememberance will be raised "We elevated your mention for
you."[94:4]
The prophet muhammed has been the most praised person in history as
around the world billions read every day (wa ash hadu anna

muhammadan abduhuu waa rasooluh) "I bear witness that Muhammad is the messenger of God"
The name Muhammed is given to most amount of children across the globe.

Chapter 11)Kalyug.

The Kalyug and the emergence of Kali According to Ved vyasa the author of the Mahabharata and the puranas and learned man of vedic knowledge Krishna made certain predictions about the future of the world to Arjuna on the battlefeild of Kurukshetra how in the coming age of man which will be the last age for humanity,the world will get corrupted and societies will change drastically some of the predictions are the following.
In kalyug a mans wealth will determine a mans good birth,good behaviour and high moral values,and the law of justice will only depend on a mans power the ones who are powerfull will get away with crimes while the ones who dont have power and wealth will suffer in silence without recieving justice.
Religion,truthfulness,cleanliness,tolerance,mercy, duration of life and memory will deminish day by day with the powerfull influence of the kaliyug.
Men and women will live together only for a Superficial attraction as we see in todays society its a common phenomena for a man and woman to live together just for fullfilling there lusts which is one of the human sins and a weakness and was something unheard of for the previous generation.
Business will depend on deception.
Womanliness and manliness will be judged by a persons sexual experience.
A man will be known as a Brahman just for using a thread.
As the earth will be filled with corruption whoever shows themselves to be the strongest will attain political power.
A persons spiritial position will be determined by external symbols and objects.
Someone who is very intelligent and uses manupilation to decieve peaple will be considered a scholar.
Children wont take care of there elderly parents.
Filling the belly will be the goal of life.
Someone who is bold and uses loudwords will be considered truthfull.
The principals of religion will be observed only for the sake of reputation.
The cities will be dominated by thieves and the Vedas will be contaminated and forgotten and athestic ideas will prevail.
Political leaders will exploit citizens.
So called preists and intellectuals will devote themselves to there bellies and gentitals
Servants will abandon a master who has lost there wealth even if the master is a holy person of exemplary character.
The duration of life for human beings in kalyug will be fifty years.
Men will kill each other over a few coins forgetten all freindships and relaions among each other.
Uncultured men will accept charity in the name of the lord.

Humans will earn a living by pretending to be beggers and wearing
such outfits.
Those who have no knowledge about religion will rise to high
positions and presume to prech about religious matters.
And as we see in todays world all of this predictions have come
true.

After the Mahabharata the Pandavas ruled for many years in peace and
prosperity till krishna left this world and they too didnt want to
remain without the guidence of krishna and all the brothers with
there common wife Draupadi left for the himalayas crowning Parikshit
as the young emperor,Parikshit was the son Abhimanyu and the
grandson of Arjuna.
As the Pandavas climbed the himalayas to attain spirutuality and
leave this world they were joined by Yamraj(Death) in the form of a
dog and soon starting with draupadi and ending with bheem all the
Pandavas left this world other than Yudishtir all of them were sent
to hell to redeem there sins and Yamraj took yudistir through hell
where he saw his brothers and draupadi beinge punished for the pride
they had in there hearts as one who has pride in ones heart cant
enter heaven.After redeeming there sins they all went to heaven and
Parikshit who was well tutored by his father and grandfather ruled
with the guidence of the elders.
During his rule the Dvapara Yug ended and Kaliyug began and as
Parikshit heard about the advent of Kali in his kingdom he went out
to search for him to contain it before it created havoc in his
kingdom,On his way he saw a bull with one broken leg dragging itself
as an evil looking man kept wipping it he was angry to witness this
atrocity and went to stop the man this man claimed to be the age of
Kali and Parikshit beinge a honourable man couldnt deny someone in
need and told kali that he could dwell in taverns where wine was
drunk,In places where women of low characters lived,in gambling dens
and in slaughter houses where violence was the norm and in gold and
kali remained true to his words for a shortime till it started
dwelling in other places as well and eventually even Parikshit fell
to its influence.
One day as parikshit went hunting after spending hours roaming the
forest and not managing to hunt even one animal he came accross a
small Ashram(Hut) he went inside to find a sage in deep meditation
he was hungry and thirsty and looked around for some food and water
but couldnt find any he tried to wake the sage up but the sage was
in deep meditaion and cpmpletely unaware of his surroundings
Parikshit got frustrated angry as he had been having a very bad day
and kali who was waiting just to influence Parikshit to commit an
act of sin found the perfect opportunity, Parikshit to take out his
anger and frustration and the desire to punish the sage took a dead
snake which was lying on the ground just outside the hut and put it
around the neck of the sage and left.
The sage was the great Samika and had no idea of the events that
took place as he was in deep meditation,the kings evil act came to
light only when the son of the sage who was also a great sage came
to the hut and found the dead snake around his fathers neck he was
furious and used his powers to find the culprit and cursed the king
that he would die bitten bye the king of snakes when his father woke

up he regretted the acts of his son as it would result in the death of a great king for making one mistake,so the sage went to warn Parikshit by this time Parikshit was also regretting his actions and was thinking of ways to make amends when the sage came and warned him he thanked the sage for the warnings and started prepairing for his death passing the crown to his son he left the kingdom and took shelter near the Ganges where he started fasting and meditating on the name of the lord,many sages from far and wide came there after hearing about the kings situation it is there when a great a sage among them recited the Bhagwat geeta to the king and the others and learning about his ancestors and the teachings of his lord he found complete spirituality when the snake came and bit him and turned his body to ash it was just his physical body his soul had already merged with the creator.

In this story there are a lot of hidden meanings and lessons one can learn as we see Parikshit learns from his elders and follow there teachings to achive success in life and the afterlife so we should also try to learn from the ones who have more experience and knowledge than us in the right ways.In Parikshits rule kalyug begins and when he heard about kali who is referred as the demon who brings kalyug upon the world in his kingdom he goes out and sees kali mistreating an animal which is shown as a wrong thing to do as Parikshit is angry at this gesture then as kali asks him for a place to dwell even though Parikshit isnt fond of kali still he allows him to dwell in certain places it shows how we should help peaple in times of need even if we might not personally like them and he tells kali to dwell in five places which are mentioned above and we compare those five places with the teachings in the quran the last revelation from god to prophet Muhammed(saw) Islam says Gambling,Wearing gold,Alcohol,Adultery and violence are prohibited so as we see kali is told by parikshit to dwell in places of association with those things so the story teaches that getting involved or dwelling in those places is bad for us and we can relate it to the Quran offering the same teachings, then we see how parikshit gives into anger and how kali is influencing him and he puts the snake around the sages neck to hurt him which results in his eventual death so this teaches us that acting on impulses such as anger is never good for us and its the whispers of demons that we fall prey to by acting on feelings of anger and lastly we see that Parikshit attains spirittuality by praying to the creator and not even death affects him when he has found god and lets go off the material world this teaches us to overcome our fears we must turn to god even the greatest fear of man which is death goes away when we know we are going to a better place back to the creator from where we came from.

Chapter 12)Philistine.

Beelzebub is known as the prince of the devils in the bible which seems like a reference to the antichrist also known as Dajjal in the quran it is often assumed that the antichrist is the son of the devil like Jesus is assumed to be the son of god but if we look at most religious texts Gods words are revealed to the prophets in a metaphorical way rather than a literal meaning so son can mean a subordinate or like a general or an important figure or some other way as Jesus was a prophet and creation of god rather than his literal son but as he was born of the virgin mary christions have misleaded to believe him as the literal son of god.In the old Testament Baalzebub is the name given to the god of the Philistine city. The Philistines were a group of peaple who arrived in the Levant an area that included modern day Israel,Gaza,Lebanon and Syria during 12th century B.C they came during a time when cities and civilizations in the Middle East and Greece were collapsing and stayed till 604 BC when they were exciled to Mesopotamia. We can determine they were a violent peaple engaged in wars frequently as we see God told moses not to flee with the Isralites through there land rather cross the Red sea when they were fleeing from the Pharoh even if that rout was shorter but as peaple might get afraid from seeing the wars and run away.A funny coincidence or a horrific fact which can be related to the Philistine god beelzebub or the prince of devils is that the prophet Muhammad prophecised that Dajjal(antichrist) will claim to be a prophet at first than will proclaim himself GOD and will apear from the lands of Israel and form greater Israel but 1400 years ago at the time of the prophet there was no state known as Israel it was formed after world war 2 in 1947 so it makes us wander if there is a relation beetween the philistine god also known as the prince of devils and the prophecy of muhammad as the peaple of Philistine did reside in that area until they were exciled but could it be they have returned.

Chapter 13)Pyramids.

The egyptian Pyramids are the most mysterious structures on planet earth,there is no specific proof of when,why and by who they were built.
These structures wieght around 6 million tones with each stone weighting around 80 tons which had been transported from 500 miles away,and now unlike earlier assumptions that they were tombs have been known that were certainly not,so the question arises for what purpose were they created ?
                    Nicola Tesla
The great scientist responsible for discovering and building the core of around eighty percent of modern technology that is used today is somewhat forgetten by the world,as this great man was not running behind money and fame or material possesions but wanted to unravel the mystries of the world and the universe and did so by creating this modern world that we live in,the mobiles,TV,cars and mostly all of discoveries concerning electricity are somehow connected to Nicola Tesla but most of us have never heard of him and are aware about Thomas Edison as the one who discovered the light bulb,but Thomas Edison had Tesla working for him and later stole Teslas discoveries these are controversies and truths about the world which remain untold as we understand history is filled with the opinions of the ones in power not the truth.
Nicola Tesla believed that the pyramids served a greater purpose and was studying them.

"The day science begins to study non-physical phenomena,it will make
more progress in one decade than in all the previous centuries of
its existence" Nicola Tesla qouted.
He submitted a paper to study the art of transmitting elecrical
energy through the natural medium,it included designs for a series
of worldwide generators,Tesla realized that the ionosphere was
sparkling with electrical energy which could easily be tapped,planet
earth according to Tesla was a gigantic electrical generator
spinning around two magnetic poles from which limitless energy can
be harnessed,using the right medium or shape his device was later
reffered to as Teslas electromagnetic pyramid based on his design
looking like a triangle shape.Pyramids exhibit a fractal energy much
more efficiently than other types of designs but more than the
actual shape it was the location of the Pyramids that created the
power and he created his facility in colarado in line with pyramids
of Giza which were an elliptical orbit of the earth and on those
sites had some realtion with the equator which was connected to the
magnetic feild of the earth,so he believed he could transfer energy
wirelessly.Modern mobile towers which transmit electrical signals to
the ionosphere of the earth and from there they bounce to another
location and transmit the signals,according to Nicola Tesla 369 is a
key to a universe.Humans have not created Mathematics but discovered
it is the language of the universe and law no matter where you are
in the universe.
There are tales in the ancient Sumerian texts about saven sages who
came before the flood and gifted mankind with civilisation and
technology,these sages are also known as immortals or gods,the
Sumerian and Egyptian gods have great similarities and are
considered the same differenly viewed by different
civilisations.Osiris or Inki is the leader and is said to have
Amphibian genes,and is killed by nemesis Seth who is Allele in both
Sumerian and Egyptian mythology.All of Osiris servants were
slaughtered in the Aquatic temple of Osiris.Then there is Isis the
godess Ninti in the Sumerian texts who is working for the
resurrection of Osiris and creates Horus by the genetic code of
Osiris,Modern Science has recently proved that everyone has a
genetic code and in the near future they can genetically modify
human babies to give them certain characteristics they have named it
disigner babies,this feild of research is known as CRISPR.Another
example of the past and future colliding with one another.She
created the great Pyramids to carry out this task.There are many
geometrical numbers associated these structures which give out the
golden ratio,The earths circumferance and many of the dimentions of
our planet and its allignment with the stars,so are all these just
coincidenses or are these structures trying to explain to us about
certain greater realities of the world and the afterlife.If the
tribe of Osiris survived after flood and were the ones responsible
for advancements in civilisation and considered themselves to be
gods so there is another connection with this tribe and another one
of our conspiracies about the Illuminati, where a theorist claims
that the major bloodline connected with the house of David with the
blood of Lucifer running through there veins,and have ancient
connections to a tribe in Egypt which migrated to the British
Isles,what is true ? what is false ? our lord knows better.

The Annunaki

There are some texts in which it is said the Annunaki or the seven sages or gods in the Sumerian litreture are ancient beings who genetically modified humans to make them smarter,so that humans could work for them they created the Egyptian Pyramids to harvest energy and they were intrested in harvesting the Gold,this connection is also made to the Illuminati who are intrested in harvesting gold and consider themselves superior than the rest of society.

Adam the first man

Our species began with our common forefather Adam who was said to be as large as four football feilds and was given all the knowledges of the heavenly realms,he was so noble and bestowed with such knowledge that god told all the angels and Ginns to bow in front of him in respect,but Iblis also known as the devil decided not to bow as he considered Adam to be inferior to him,the human species were given earth over the Ginn kind who were the rulers before the humans,so Iblis asked god to grant him time till the end of the human realm and he will show god that humans are a corrupted species and will disobey god,so it is revealed in the Quran that"O children of Adam iblis is your enemy do not disobey god and fall to the tricks of the devils."

So it is believed that humans had far superior knowledge in the past then they posses now,so they had access to greater technology as well,this can be related to many of the tales from different parts of the world in all the older religions the ones which came before the flood and in the Mythological studies and ancient tales we find tales humans who were a highly advanced civilisation possesing heavenly powers and knowledge.

Chapter 14)September 11th and Islamophobia.

The september 11 attacks,often referred to as 9/11 were a series of four cordinated bomb blasts on the twin towers of the world trade centre were many innocents lost there lives and there was a property damage of around ten billion dollars.This was done by the Al-Qaeda organisation,who had raged war on America or were retaliating for the Americans causing destruction to the Islamic world.

This was the beginning of the war on Terror by America in which the CIA were given authorisation by the goverment to hunt down and kill the Al-Qaeda leadership with Osama bin Laden at the head of the organisation and the most wanted man in the world.

The CIA and the American forces were on there way creating havoc and destruction on the Islamic world,this paved the path to the war on Iraq.Pakistan beinge there major ally in hunting down the so called terrorists who had made there way in the mountain terrains which would be very hard to infiltrate by the American forces,So America hired the Afghani war lords to fight there battle but these were the peaple who had fought alongside Osama bin-Laden against the soviets in which America were helping them,these peaple considered Osama there hero and a freedom fighter for the Islamic world so they would not kill Osama rather take the money of the Americans and put up a show.All this was happening under the Bush Administration,George

W.Bush wrote in his autobiography,"In my senior year I joined Skull
and Bones,a secret society,so secret,I cant say anything more".The
skull and bones organisation a secret society associated with the
Illuminati,also known as the The order or the brotherhood of Death
is an undergraduate senior secret student society at Yale University
in New Haven,Connecticut.There are rumours that this organisation
plays the same role as the Illuminati in gaining global power,the
children of the most influential families attend these universities
all of them go on to become peaple in power over resources,land and
manpower so these organisations hire and train them in there ways
through these associations and later on these peaple go on to take
part in what is known as the Agenda 21 in which a few want to have
complete control over the many to set up a one world goverments this
is the recruting methods used by such organisaions.It is also
claimed they have complete influence over the CIA.While the war on
terror was going on and America was hunting the Al-Qaeda suddenly
everything changed and Goerge Bush declared war on Iraq to overthrow
Saddam Hussein and the Al-Qaeda were forgotten and Iraq was in
turmoil the American forces after overthrowing the leadership turned
against the civilians and started mistreating and killing and
humiliating the peaple,this gave the uprising in which local armed
militias came up and the peaple welcomed the Al-Qaeda and a
defensive Jihad was called by Osama bin-Laden as an infidel country
was attacking an muslim country without any reasonable
cause.Eventually the Al-qaeda leadership in Iraq led by a warlord
known as Abu-Hamza turned the war against the Americans towards its
own peaple where he wanted to destroy the Shia community and this
turned to a civil war in the State.
The controversies regarding the begining of all these events which
led to war and destruction going on till date is that the Bush
administration and the CIA were involved or atleast knew about the
attack before it happened.The whole attack is claimed by some to be
a initiating spark used by the elites to gather the masses of the
peaple in support of the war on Islam and begin the Islamophobia all
over the world which eventually some day will lead to the third
world war according to Albert Pikes plan of the three world wars.
Jordanian intelligence,Egyptian intelligence,Israel,Uk all had been
warning the Americans and CIA about the coming attacks and the
terrorist cell working over there but the CIA denied to act on the
issue as they stated the terrorists were living on a green card on
American soil.If the attack was staged by the American elites and
the Zionists to manipulate the peaple in support of the war it
worked perfectly and is still going on in the world.Gaddafi once
said the Zionists will come after us one by one as they cant take on
everyone at the same time and wanted to create a currency based in
gold countering the American dollar and he was declared a dictator
and was removed and killed by the war on Libya,till date the country
is in complete destruction were innocents die of hunger and war
everyday so is Afghanistan,Iraq,Syria and Yemen so every country
which America goes to save ends up beinge completely destroyed so
America really needs to reconsider what they consider saving one
more time.

Chapter 15)Technology X

Human beings from the time we were created in all the heavenly
scriptures bestowed upon human kind we have been told about one
power of the heavens,that god knows everything in your mind and
heart most non believers would say thats not possible how can
someone read minds ?,but with the modern technological age the world
is changing what was considered impossible and science fiction is
possible and happening,modern science is racing ahead of science
fiction in todays world,yet most of us still are consumed by the
deceptions of the material world are unable to see the realities
unfolding in front of us.Companies such as the Silocon valley giants
and modern day technological jesus as he is known Elon musks company
Tesla have been working on brain computer interface in which they
can read the human mind using the magnetic waves generated by our
mind whenever a thought occurs in our mind computers can pick up
these signals and transform them into words,it is possible to
control prosthetic arms,computers even communicate directly with
another person just by using our minds.But if these technologies are
used in the wrong ways,every human that is living in the planet what
if there brains are accessed without even them knowing about it,what
happens to basic human privacy.The Agenda 21 also known as the plan
to create an one world goverment by the UN and other world
organisations is becoming more of a reality by using such
technology.There is a controversy behind the coming of the 5G
towers,these towers are installed to increase the speed of network
connectivity,but what if these towers and sattelites have another
purpose to have a greater access to information inside the human
brain,could it be that it is beinge used to create a record off all
human beings.In a movie Captain America the winter soldier Hollywood
showed a technology which was a sattelite having a record of all
human beings and could terminate human beings who transgress or go
against the authorities.How close is these fictional movies to our
realities or are these just ways of portraying future events to get
a greater acceptance by the public when put into effect.This
technology can even create greater virtual realities in which the
real world and the virtual world would be hard to distinguish from.
What happens when machines are used in industries and companies
robots operated by AI to do the work more effeciently than
humans,what happens to the growing human population ?.These are
questions that are not beinge answered or even thought about by most
of our countries and leaders,The corporate giants who openly support
depopulation and think they will be helping humanity by decreasing
the population so that the rest of humanity can have a greater
life.The coming times are going to have changes beyond our
imaginations so its time to prepare and pick a side and stick to it
do we choose be on the side of love and peace and our religious
values,or fall prey to hate and war and to the false ideas of
modernity and prosperity.

Chapter 16)The ten major signs.

                    "The Ten major Signs"

The ten major signs of the end of time and earth are revealed by god
to prophet Muhammed(saw) through revelations in the Hadiths we find
that after all the minor signs have come and gone over a period of
time the major signs will be unleashed upon the world the major
signs will come one after another in a short span of time but we are
not told the sequence in which they will occure the major signs are
the following :-

The Beast.
The smoke.
The coming of Dajjal(Antichrist).
The second coming of Jesus, Isa(AS).
Yajuj and Majuj(Gog and Magog).
The sun rising from the West.
Three land slides one in the East,
One in the West,
One in the Arabian Peninsula,
Fire will erupt from Yemen.

And humanity will face Judgement.

Chapter 17)Yemen.

" Civil War"

Republic of Yemen a country in the southern end of the Arabian
Peninsula where a civil war has been going on since 2015,The country
is in ruins with differnt political and military groups engaged in
conflict as a result of a proxy war going on between Saudi Arabia
and Iran.Saudi Arabia is a country looked upto by most muslims all
over the world as it is home to the,holy sites of Makkah and Madina
but the modern Saudi goverment ruled by the crown prince MD bin
Salman which has not been functionting as a rightous state following
gods words. The Saudi royal family spends millions of dollars on
personal unnessary luxiries which is forbidden by the teachings of
the Quran,The princes father King Salman was responsible for
starting the bombings on Yemen and countless war crimes against the
country which are still going on, almost a 100,000 civilians have
lost there lives including woman and children.
Iran as one of the biggest Shia powers in the region is trying to
have dominance over the region by supporting the Houthis who are
Shia Muslims,Saudi Arabia has a majority of Sunni Muslims and the
Saudi Monarchy has been known to oppress and discriminate against
the minority groups of Shia Muslims.To understand the root of these
differences between the shia and sunni muslims we have to go back to
632 AD after the death of prophet Muhammad there was a conflict
regarding who should be the successor as caliph,Sunnis believed
muhammads successor should be Abu bakr and Oman and Shias believed
it should be Ali this resulted in the first civil conflicts within
the Muslim ummah,and can be traced to the modern times where civil
war is destroying countries such as Yemen and Syria,one of the most
important prophecies of prophet muhammad regarding the end times are
civil wars among the muslims and in the world,the cold war and the
modern day proxy wars beinge fought between these powerful countries

beinge controlled by a minority of elites ruling over them can be
seen as the prophecy coming true and the world moving closer to the
end.

Part-C
Chapter 1)Prophet Ayyub AS.

Ayuub(AS) Job the son Razeek
Once upon a time when the angels were sitting in Jannah and they
gathered together to discuss,who was the most beloved servant to
allah azzawajal and at that time they came up with a name of a great
prophet,he had a quality he would thank Allah(SWT) upon all
conditions,this prophet was tested in every way possible but he was
always patient,indeed he was often returning to us he was none other
than the prophet Ayyus (AS).He was a decendant of prophet
Abraham(AS) his wife was one of the direct decendants of the prophet
Yusuf(AS).
Ayyub(AS) was sent to Hurran which is the south of Syria.He was very
rich with livestock and land,he had fourteen children.He was a
community leader Allah wanted to see weather he would be thankfull
if all his riches will be taken away from him.
And with time he lost everything but he was still thanking Allah,ya
Allah,I praise you upon all conditions,he never complained,Then
Iblis came to Ayyub(AS) as a human and said look at you,your praying
everyday yet what is your prayer doing for you look what happened
you lost everything what kind of lord is this for you so
Ayyub(AS)replied Allah gives to whom he wills and takes from who he
wills.All the wealth I have belongs to Allah so he has every right
to take it from me.Allah decided to test him further so all the
souls of his children were taken all fourteen.With the death of
every child he would say we all belong to Allah,whatever he has
given to us was always his,if he took it away it just returns to
whom it belongs to he says Allah knows this test would be good for
me,so it is bestowed upon me so he thanks Allah and keeps praising
Allah.Then Allah decides to test him further his health is taken
away from him,he becomes in a condition where his skin starts
falling apart and his internal organs start rotting ,the peaple of
his community start saying he is a bad person or else Allah wouldnt
have punished him this way,his close freinds and community stayed
away from him as had no money his wife started cooking in other
peaples house to feed Ayyub(AS) but peaple didnt want his wife to
cook in there houses thinking she might infect them so she lost her
job.Ayyub(AS) had suffered for eighteen years as they had no food
and no money,one day Ayyub(AS) wife decided to cut off some off of
her hair to sell it and buy some food to feed Ayyub(AS),she was
asked by him where did you get the money from she didnt reply the
next day she cut of the rest of her hair to buy food,this time when
she came back Ayyub(AS)insisted where did you get the money from as
her head was covered he couldnt see,She removed the scarf from her
head and seeing her head bold Ayyub(AS) broke up from the inside
understanding that she sold her hair to feed him.He fell down on his
knees and made a dua to Allah for help,he didnt blame Allah he just
asked to be saved from the evils which have fallen upon him.Till now
he had never asked anything he kept praising Allah throughout his

difficult times.Allah answered his dua he was instructed to hit his
foot in the ground and water came out Allah told him to wash his
body and drink from the water and his body healed,his wife was made
eightteen years younger they had twenty eight children and much more
money and wealth then they had before,Allah considered him the best
in ways.

Chapter 2)Frog and the well.

                    The frog in the well
Once upon a time there was a frog that lived in a well he had grew
up in the well and had no idea about the existance of the outside
world,he was the only frog in that well he had a good life lots of
bugs lived there he ate them and grew fat and was fullfilled with
his life and considered himself the king of the world as he thought
that the well was the whole world and he was the most superior
beinge inside the well.One day another frog that lived in the sea
was hopping around and by mistake fell inside the well he met the
frog in the well and they started talking "where did you come
from?"asked the frog of the well the other frog replied that he came
from the sea which was huge and filled with so many things that was
beyond the imagination of this frog and asked the frog to come with
him to the sea but this frog in his ignorance replied "there cant be
anything greater than this well your just trying to fool me"that
frog didnt say anything and left and this frog stayed in the well
and never will he ever know about the true realities and vastness of
the world as he considered the well his whole world.This story was
narrated by Swami Vivekananda to make peaple understand that it is
our naive thinking that we consider this earth our whole world and
there are realities beyond our imagination in the heavenly kingdoms
and if we behave like the frog then we might as well perish without
ever knowing and experiencing those realities in the afterlife.

Chapter 3)The three boons.

                    The three Boons
Once upon a time there was a young man named Haru in a village far
away he was short and had a small nose,he worked very hard everyday
but earned very little as he was not educated but his mother loved
him and took care of him,everyone in the village made fun of Haru
because of his small nose,he felt sad and hurt but didnt slash out
at them took the insults quietly.Then as time went by his mother
passed away and Haru became very sad,he was advised by an elder to
get married to get rid of his sadness but he was afraid that he
shouldnt marry a very pretty girl as she would also make fun of
him,so he went and told the elder to find him such a girl,So the
elder found a girl who also had a small nose in a nearby village and
got Haru married to her,they were very happy and Haru thought all
his problems would go away but things only got worse as now the
villagers made fun of them both as the small nosed couple,Haru

pleaded to them to stop and even went to the elders to ask for help
but nothing worked so he turned to god and thought only his creator
could get him out of this situation,so he went to the forest and
started meditating on the name of the lord.He prayed all day all
night without even moving till god sent an angel with a messege to
give to Haru that god had given him three boons and gave him a pair
of dice to throw and ask for his wish,Haru went to his wife and gave
her the good news she thought that they should ask for wealth but
Haru decided they should ask for beautiful noses instead so he threw
the dice and asked for beautiful noses there whole bodies were
covered with noses,they were both horrified to look at each others
body and then he asked for the noses to be removed and they became
noseless,so he prayed again and as his third wish asked for his
original noses back as they though what will they do with wealth
without there noses.

Moral-Opportunity once lost may not come again one should make use
of the opportunities in the best way they can.

Chapter 4)Swami Vivekananda.

                    Swami vivekananda
Swami Vivekananda, a famous Saint from India, was lovingly called
Biley in his childhood years. One of the games Biley and his friends
enjoyed was a competition to see who meditates the longest. All the
children would sit with their eyes closed and each one would think
of his favorite deity.

One day, when they were playing this game, one of them heard a soft
sound. As he opened his eyes, he saw a big snake slithering towards
them. The boy started shouting, "Cobra! Cobra!" On hearing that, all
of them except Biley, got up and ran away. Even as they ran, they
shouted warnings, "Biley, come away! Hurry up; there is a big cobra
approaching. It will bite you, Run! Run!" But Biley did not hear
their shouts. He was sitting with his eyes closed, thinking only of
God. He was enjoying Bliss, completely unaware of the commotion
around him.

And what do you think the cobra did? The cobra reared up, spread its
hood and watched Biley for some time. Then slowly it bowed to Biley
and slithered away without touching or disturbing him. The story
about the cobra leaving Biley alone spread rapidly, with Biley's
friends narrating it excitedly to his parents as well as his
neighbours. They were awed by the divine protection Biley had
acquired through his intense concentration and love for God.

Chapter 5)The accident.

                    The accident
It takes two hours from guwahati to shilong "close the window im
freezing" john said, it was a cold moonless night the sky was dark

and low our cars headlight paved the way up the swirly hills, on the
top rested the city of shilong,I closed the window,As feelings of
adventure and freedom burst through my veins, Rahul was sitting in
the front rolling a joint "the best marijuana in India grows on the
top of this mountain" he said with a smirk "dont smoke in the car"
said john "dont be a killjoy john" rahul replied as he lit the joint
"want to smoke shoaib?" rahul asked passing me the joint i took it
and took a puff, as i exhaled the smoke Baaam! a sound came the car
had hit something the joint flew off my hand as the car drifted and
came to a stop."What was that?" john asked we got down there was a
shadowy object lying on the road, i took out my phone and turned the
flashlight on "aaahh"shouted John there was a women drenched in a
pool of blood laying on the road, I started walking back horrified
at the sight, I tripped and fell down everything went dark."Shoiab
get up"Rahul was shaking me, I opened my eyes sitting in the car it
seemed i was hallucinating,I felt a sence of relief "you passed
out"rahul said laughing,suddenly we stopped "look over there"rajesh
our driver was pointing to a white marble monument shining in the
dark "thats the tomb of Natalia she died in an accident on this road
they say her spirit still haunts these roads" "dont try to scare
us"rahul said laughing as I sat quietly as my blood ran cold.

Chapter 6)The gift.

                    "The gift"
The trees were glimsing with the morning dew as the birds flew in
and out of them the suns light shined on the green grass as men and
women jogged on the paved roads while some children played on the
park swing,I was sitting on the bench overlooking the lake "Shoaib
want to go ride a boat"asked john he was sitting next to me we
studied at the same school and were meeting after a long time as all
schools were closed due to the corona virus."No lets just sit here"i
replied "why do you look so dull?"expressed john, "Im fine" I
muttered as the thought swiped through my head that my father had
lost his job due to the lockdown and i still didnt have my books for
school as my family was barely making ends meet,"im excited about
school I told my dad to buy me the new Iphone 11 im bored of using
this one"john said with a smirk on his face "didnt you buy your
phone this year only just be grateful for what you have" I
elaborated "Keep your rightousness to yourself and have a donut"john
said laughing as he took out couple of donuts from a picnic basket
and handed me one "lets go our dads must be coming any time to pick
us up"i stated as i got up and walked towards the main entrance john
followed as we reached the gate a car pulled over "get in"shouted
Johns dad from inside "see you in school shoaib"babbled john,I
nodded in acknowledged as he drove away uncertain If I was going to
going back to school.As I looked around I saw my dad walking towards
me "salam malikum" he professed "malikum assalam" I emphasised "did
you have a good time"yes I replied,he smiled as he passed me a box
wrapped and tied with a ribbon "this is for you" he said "Thanks
what is it ?"i questioned while opening the box,Inside I found new
books for my school, my heart filled with happiness and my eyes

puffed up with tears "but where did you get money from?"I asked
confused "i keep a secret piggy bank saving money for your
future"dad replied with a smile as I threw myself into his arms.

Chapter 7)Prophet Yunus AS.

Yunus(AS)Jonah

His whole Ummah accepted the messege.He is also known as the Dhan
Nun the companion of the big fish.He was sent to Nineveh it is in
northern Iraq very near to todays Masul with a population of one
hundred thousand.Peaple rejected Yonus,he warned the peaple that
Allah will punish them,the peaple were unhappy with him and harsh to
his,he got frustrated and left to find other peaple because he
wanted to go spread the deen but Allah didnt tell him to go,he made
a mistake by leaving without permision from Allah,he went to the sea
and boarded a ship and while at sea a storm came the ship started
sinking the peaple decided in order for them to survive they needed
to get rid of there luggage so they threw the there luggage in the
sea but the ship kept sinking,so they decided they needed to throw a
passenger overboard they decided to do a lucky draw and as it came
on Yunus they decided not to throw him as he was a humble,kind
blessed man,so they decided to draw again but it came on Yunus once
more they said No!No!No we wont get rid of Yunus,this is our
Barakah,this is our blessing on the boat.The third time they drew
but again it landed on Yunus(AS)now he understood it was from Allah
so he said Bismillah hir rahman nir raheem(In the name of allah the
most merciful the entirely merciful) and jumped off the ship.Allah
commanded the whale the big fish to swallow him whole and the whale
came and swallowed him.It is said Sayyidina Yunus (AS) was
unconscious and woke up inside the stomach of the whale and thought
he was in the grave as he didnt see the whale swallowing him,but as
he touched around he understood this wasnt the grave but the stomach
of a whale,the acid inside a whales stomach is twelve times stronger
than that of a human digestive system.Yunus(AS) skin started to peel
off and he was hearing some voices he wandered what it was and O
Allah what is that i hear ? Thats the fish and pebbles making
tasbih.Then the realisation hit him and he started making sujood and
said Allah im making Sujood where no one else has made sujood to you
before in the stomach of a whale and then made his famous Dua
recorded in the Quran he called out in the three darknesses,The
stomach of the whale,the darkness inside the sea,and and the
darkness of the night.The dua was "La ilaha illa anta subhana kainni
kuntu mil allah ali meen"
None has the right to be worshipped but you,glorified and exalted be
you truly I have been of the wrong doers.This is the Dua of
distress.
How long he stayed in the stomach of the whale is uncertain from
three to forty days ,the week voice of Yunus(AS) was heard by the
angels in the heavens they went to allah and asked isnt that our
regular worshipper asking for help Allah said yes and they answered
his dua.He was saved as he remembered Allah in moments of ease so he

was saved in difficulty.We need to remember Allah in our young age
so Allah remembers us in our old age.
Remember Allah when your healthy so Allah will remember you when
your ill.Remember Allah while you live so Allah will remember you
when you die.
The whale was ordered by Allah to swim to the shore and spit him out
the whale vomitted him on the shore.But Yunus (AS) did not have skin
to protect him from the sunlight,wind then Allah ordered a tree to
grow over Yunus(AS), so it will shade him feed him while he rested
and recovered.But now Yunus(AS)had to finish his task so he returned
to his peaple and was shocked as when he had left punishment was
hovering over them,his nation saw these signs of darkness,dark
clouds coming over them unnatural at odd times,they had heard the
stories of the peaple of the past Nations beinge destroyed after the
prophets left so they got scared and repented back to Allah,all of
them were crying all of them believed the only Prophet whose whole
nation accepted the messege.

Chapter 8)Prophet Zakarya(AS) and Yahya(AS).

Zakarya(AS) a great prophet comes from the decendants of Dawood and
Sulaiman(AS),at his time he would lead the prayers,he was close to
Zakarya he was very pious and known as Imran.Zakarya(AS)was sent to
Bani Israel.Al-Imran are the decendants of Ibraheem(AS) and the
family of Isa(AS).
The wife of Imran one day praying to Allah saw a bird going and
feeding her babies carrying the food in her beak and as the wind
blew she hid her babies with her wings,seeing this she felt the
desire to have a child at that age,she said Allah give me a
child,bless us!my husband is leading the peaple in prayer we are
serving you the best we can.Allah answered the dua but Allah
dictates in the Quran that she had made a pledge to us that the
child in her womb will be dedicated in the service of Allah.
Which meant that the child will be serving in the masjid of Al-
Aqsa,as she had the child it was a female so as traditionally at
that times females could not serve in the Masjid,Allah says Allah
knows better what she delivered and then Allah says the male is not
like the female,This means Allah is saying whatever male child you
have delivered would not be better than the female,Allah has given
you.As the female Allah has given you is the best in the world.She
dosent know Allah knows better,this female is Maryam(AS),The father
passed away when the mother was pregnant,Sheikh Imran and there was
a debate as to who would take care of this child,the preists and the
religious peaple all wanted the right.They drew a lottery all of
them put there pens and made a child come and pick a pen and the
child picked the pen of Zakarya(AS) and they said no,they said no we
have to try again.
Now they put there pens in a little wooden basket and said whoevers
flow the other way will be chosen and Zakarya(AS) was the only one
this was the second sign,the peaple said no lets try again whoevers
flows with the stream will be picked,Now Allah made it so that only
Zakarya(AS)flowed with the stream,So Zakarya(AS) took her to take

care of her,but Zakarya was the Imam of the house of Allah in order
for him to take care of the child she had to stay in the Masjid all
the time.
She was kept in a little room of worship known as Al-
Mihrab,everytime Zakarya(AS) went there she was engaged in worship
she was a person dedicated to the house of worship,she was the most
pious women even when she was just a child and at times she had
fruit of different seasons totally fresh,this kept happening
repeatedly,So Zakarya(AS) asked "who gave you this?"as this is
impossible to have at this time of the year in Jerusalem she replied
"ALLAH".
Allah gives the ones he wishes without any limit,there were miracles
that were happening at that time all the time,So Zakarya (AS)
thought if Allah could give anything which he already knew then he
should ask for children as at his old age and his wifes age she
could not bear children anymore,So he made a dua Allah grant me a
pious child,"OH! my lord my bones are weak my hair is grey but,I
shall keep praying to you,He was worried that after him there was no
one to lead the peaple in the religious affairs of Bani
Israel,therefore he wanted to have a child.This dua was accepted the
angels called him,"We are giving you a child and he shall be named
Yahya or John nobody before him has had that name,Allah named him
and gave him certain qualities that no one before him
had,Zakarya(AS) was shocked so he asked Allah for a sign as his wife
was barren and Allah said "You shall not speak to any mankind for
three days" so he started giving peaple orders to obey Allah by
signs and after three days recieved the news of his wifes
pregnancy,and this child will be the great prophet Yahya(AS).The
Torah was repeated to him and he memorised it,Yahya (AS) was young
and was going to be the prophet of Bani Israel who were peaple gone
corrupt,So Allah gave him judgement and wisdom when he was very
young,We made him to love all humans and other cretures of Allah.He
was a serious child from ayoung age he used to read and worship not
play and joke around like the other children,we also purified him in
all ways.He did not marry he was dedicated to the religion.He
recieved the five commadments,Allah told Isa (AS) that either he
conveys them or you convey them,So Isa(AS) told him either you
either convey the messege to the peaple or I will.Yahya(AS) was
afraid that if he didnt convey the messege he would be punished so
he went forth and decided to convey the messege,Yahya(AS) gathered
the children of Jerusalem with Isa(AS) standing next to him (John
and Jesus) so he praised Allah and dictated the five commadments.
*   Worship allah alone associate no gods beside him.
*   I command you to pray while praying dont turn your face away or
    Allah will turn away from you.
*   Fastin
*   Give charity
*   Remember the name of Allah.
Zakarya(AS)was the father of Yahya(AS) they were the two main
leaders in Bani Israel,the peaple used to look up to them and
respect them,at that time there was a tyrant king who fell in love
with his neice and his neice was an evil women and they said she was
also a prostitute,and when the king fell in love with her she wanted
to be the queen but she couldnt,as it was haram in there religion,so

she sent for a fatwa to Yahya(AS) asking him is it permissible for
the king who was her uncle ?.
It was also sent to Zakarya(AS) he also said haram.
And one night as she was with her uncle she started to play on her
uncle which is the king,to attract him when he came near her she
said no its haram,she said I wont let you touch me unless you get me
Yuhya(AS)head as dowry,the king hyped up in desires ,arrogance and
pride sent his troops to Yuhya(AS) they went behind him and cut his
head off,which was brought on a golden platter to the neice and as
Zakarya(AS) objected he was also ordered to be killed as the
soldiers came for him he ran to the forest,where god sent the angels
to open up a tree to hide and save him,while he hid in the tree the
soldiers searched for him and Iblis came as a man and showed them a
cloth on the ground and said he must be hiding inside the tree the
soldiers cut down the tree and Zakarya(AS) also came to an end.